THE CHRISTIAN OLD TESTAMENT

Looking at the
Hebrew Scriptures
through
Christian Eyes

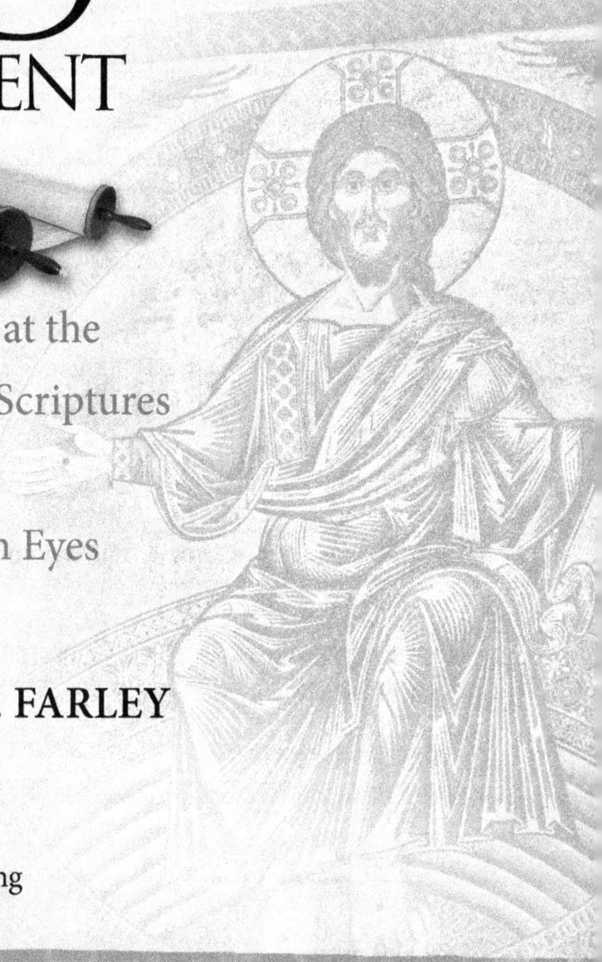

LAWRENCE R. FARLEY

Ancient Faith Publishing
Chesterton, Indiana

THE CHRISTIAN OLD TESTAMENT
Looking at the Hebrew Scriptures through Christian Eyes
Copyright © 2012 by Lawrence R. Farley

All Rights Reserved

Published by   Ancient Faith Publishing
A division of Ancient Faith Ministries
P.O. Box 748
Chesterton, IN 46304

No part of this publication may be reproduced, stored in a retrieval system, or transmitted in any form by any means, electronic, mechanical, photocopy, recording, or otherwise, without the prior written permission of the publisher, except for brief quotations in critical reviews or articles.

Unless otherwise noted, all Scripture quotations are from the New King James Version of the Bible, © 1979, 1980, 1982, 1984 by Thomas Nelson, Inc., Nashville, Tennessee, and are used by permission.

Printed in the United States of America

ISBN: 978-1-936270-53-8

30 29 28 27 26 25 24 23 22 21   11 10 9 8 7 6 5 4 3

Library of Congress Cataloging-in-Publication Data

Farley, Lawrence R.
The Christian Old Testament : looking at the Hebrew Scriptures through Christian eyes / Lawrence R. Farley.
   p. cm.
ISBN 978-1-936270-53-8 (alk. paper)
1. Bible. O.T.--Criticism, interpretation, etc. I. Title.

BS1171.3.F37 2012
221.6--dc23

2012016332

Dedicated to
Ted and Virginia Byfield,
with admiration and gratitude

CONTENTS

Preface
The "Other" Testament 7

Introduction
Reading the Old Testament as Children of the New 13

Chapter 1
Genesis: Walking with the Patriarchs 17

Chapter 2
The Law: Worshipping within the Tents 45

Chapter 3
The Historical Books: Living in the Land 73

Chapter 4
The Prophets: Listening to God 93

Chapter 5
The Writings: Singing the Lord's Song 131

Conclusion
We Have Found the Messiah 159

About the Author 165

PREFACE

THE "OTHER" TESTAMENT

WHEN I WAS IN GRADE FIVE, along with the rest of my grade five classmates, I received a New Testament (with Psalms) from the Gideons. Apparently the Gideons had an agreement with the schools that they might distribute the New Testament free of charge to all grade five school children, in much the same way as they famously placed the entire Bible free of charge in every hotel room. It is easy now to smile at the evangelical optimism of the Gideons, but my wife credits her youthful spiritual awakening to reading that grade five New Testament. (Significantly, her conversion to Christ was not complete until she spoke to her friend, who took her to her Baptist church. From my present perspective, I would say that this illustrates the Orthodox assertion that the Scriptures only bear fruit fully when read and experienced from within the Church.)

I have always wondered why the Gideons distributed only the New Testament in schools, and not the entire Bible. I imagine it had something to do with cost, since the printing and distributing of the entire Bible would cost rather more than printing and distributing the slimmer volume of the New Testament. Doubtless they felt that, given their desire to convert people to Christ through reading the Scriptures, concentrating on the New Testament gave them more bang for their limited buck. Whatever their reasoning, they are surely to be commended for their zeal and desire to convert children to the One who said that the Kingdom of Heaven belonged to such as they.

Having said that, we still need to read the entire Bible, both the New Testament and "the other Testament," especially since this "other Testament" is something of a closed book to many Christians. My guess is that many Christians begin to read with good intentions. They start on page one, as they do with any other book, plow through Genesis well enough (lots of good stories, such as the exciting tale of Joseph and his brothers), enjoy reading about Israel's deliverance from Egypt in the early chapters of Exodus (thanks perhaps largely to Charlton Heston), and then bog down considerably in the wilderness (which is where Israel also bogged down). Chapter after chapter about building the Tabernacle and its furnishings, with no pictures. Then comes Leviticus, with long descriptions about how to sacrifice animals and which parts of their guts to burn on the altar and where to put the blood, and by then it's pretty much game over. Forget about Numbers and Deuteronomy. Readers may remember stories about Joshua and the Battle of Jericho, when the walls came a-tumbling down, but it is unlikely they will get far enough into the text to read about it. The Old Testament, which for our Lord and the apostles and their Church was simply "the Scriptures," is now "the other Testament." The bookmark remains, to all intents and purposes, somewhere in Exodus.

It must be candidly admitted that our contemporary Orthodox lectionary does not help us here very much. Unlike the days of St. Justin the Philosopher and Martyr in the mid-second century, when the Old Testament was read at every Sunday Liturgy, today we do not read the Old Testament at the Liturgy. And we scarcely read it at Vespers either, though for some Great Feasts we get a quick series of three lessons. (Often the same lessons get repeated over and over again.) There are, of course, many lessons read in Holy Week. On Holy Saturday at the Liturgy of St. Basil we get fifteen Old Testament lessons. But Holy Week hardly makes up for the liturgical dearth of Old Testament reading the rest of the year.

The result of this dearth is that many Orthodox have only a passing familiarity with the Old Testament, and are therefore unable to appreciate our rich hymnography, which presupposes an intimate familiarity with it. If you doubt this, try this experiment: go up to any Orthodox (especially one who is not a convert from the evangelical churches) and quote the hymn about the Mother of God that is sung when the bishop arrives: "The prophets proclaimed you from on high, O Virgin: the Jar, the Staff, the Candlestick, the Table, the Uncut Mountain, the Golden Censer, the Tabernacle, the Gate Impassible, the Palace, the Ladder, and the Throne of kings."

Then ask the person to explain why the hymn calls the Mother of God "the Jar." Or "the Staff." Or "the Uncut Mountain," or any of the other images. My guess is that he will not have the faintest clue, and will not be able to identify the passages of the Old Testament from which these typological images are drawn. Indeed, if the first person you ask promptly answers, "The Jar? Oh, that's from Exodus 16, and she's called 'the Jar' because the manna was placed in the jar in the same way as Christ the Bread of Heaven dwelt in her," then I will be very surprised. My own experience is that most Orthodox are quite unfamiliar with these Old Testament stories, and so could not make the identifications the writer of the hymn clearly assumed his hearers could make.

The pressing need, therefore, is to gain a familiarity with the Old Testament, and that is not just to enhance our understanding of our Orthodox hymnography. More importantly, we need a familiarity with the Old Testament in order to understand more fully the New Testament. The challenges, questions, and controversies of the New Testament are all rooted in the Old Testament experiences of Israel, and if we lack this historical context, we will miss much of the richness of Christ's interactions with His contemporaries and of the teaching of His apostles. Reading the New Testament while remaining ignorant of the Old would be like trying to understand the Protestant Reformation without first understanding the Western Middle Ages. In New Testament interpretation as well as in church history, historical context is crucial.

The apostles spent much of their time teaching their first converts the correct understanding of the Scriptures and how they were fulfilled in Jesus of Nazareth. And when the apostles moved out of Jerusalem and Judea into a Gentile environment, they immediately began the process of educating these newly converted Gentiles in the literature of the Jewish people. Conversion to the God of Israel and His Jewish Messiah meant possession of and education in the Jewish Scriptures. That is why

"Christian anti-Semitism," where it exists, is not just moronic, but also oxymoronic. Christianity is spiritually Jewish.

The Church, therefore, read the Old Testament to its converts, strove to make them familiar with the Law and the Prophets as well as with the Gospels and the Epistles, and it early presupposed this familiarity. Take, for example, the letter of St. Clement of Rome, written to the Gentile church of Corinth at about the end of the first century. When he writes to exhort them to be humble, he does not do what we think would be the obvious thing and quote from the New Testament about the virtues of humility. Rather, he quotes extensively from the Old Testament, assuming his hearers know these stories and will get his point. It was not the case that the Church stuck to the New Testament Scriptures and left the Old Testament to Jews or even to Jewish Christians. The Old Testament, equally with the New, was the property of the Church, the New Israel.

In this book, I will begin with an Introduction, explaining the basic Christian approach to the Old Testament. I will then look at the different books of the Old Testament in all their variety, offering general introductions and explanations of the passages so they can be understood in their original context. I will especially focus on passages in those books that speak directly about Christ, trying to convey why these passages had such resonance for Christians, and also what devotional value Christians can derive from them today. I will conclude by presenting the Christian case for the Church's use of the Old Testament as more compelling than the classic Jewish use of those Scriptures. My aim is to restore the Old Testament to the hearts of Christian readers as a Christian book, and to increase their love and familiarity with the stories our Lord and His apostles read and loved.

Note: Throughout this work, the Hebrew text will be used, as well as the Hebrew numbering of the Psalter (so that Psalm 23 is the shepherd psalm). A number of biblical references will be given. These should be looked up and read, rather than treated simply as numerical footnotes.

References to the Septuagint numbering, where different, will be given in parentheses. The names of the books of the Bible in the Septuagint Greek translation (as in the *Orthodox Study Bible*) differ somewhat from the more customary names of the books as found in other Bibles. The following chart shows the differences.

1 Samuel = 1 Kingdoms
2 Samuel = 2 Kingdoms
1 Kings = 3 Kingdoms
2 Kings = 4 Kingdoms
Ezra = 2 Ezra
1 Esdras = 1 Ezra

INTRODUCTION

READING THE OLD TESTAMENT AS CHILDREN OF THE NEW

IN THE EARLY DAYS OF THE SECOND CENTURY, St. Ignatius, bishop of Antioch, was on his way to die. He had been arrested for being a Christian (being the pastor of the church in the third largest city of the Roman Empire, he was hard to miss), and was on his way to Rome to be executed. While on his long way there, he wrote letters to several Christian communities.

In one of them, his letter to the church in Philadelphia, he referred to an argument he once had with some people in that city. The exact nature of the argument is unclear, but what is clear is that his opponents referred to the Jewish Scriptures, the charter library we call "the Old Testament." They thought that Ignatius's teaching could not be proven from this charter, and they said, "If I do not find it in the charter, I will not believe it in the Gospel." Ignatius insisted, "It *is* written there," in the Old Testament, and they retorted, "Well, *that's* the question, isn't it." The argument was about the teaching of the Gospels, and Ignatius's opponents were saying that something had to be clearly present in the Old Testament before they would believe it in the New. Then Ignatius said something revealing.

"As for me," the bishop of Antioch said, "my charter is Jesus Christ, the inviolable charter is His Cross, and His Death and His Resurrection."

13

In this statement, more like a *riposte* than a considered theological doctrine, we find the whole Christian understanding of the Old Testament. In a word, the Christians read the Old Testament as a revelation of Christ. It is not the case that Christians read the Old Testament, clearly understand everything in it and how it all fits together, and then look at Jesus' words and ministry to see whether or not it all stacks up with that understanding. The Old Testament does not enlighten and validate Jesus so much as He enlightens and validates it. He is the foundation, the basis on which we Christians understand the Old Testament and everything else. He is the charter.

That is because there is much in the Old Testament that is, if not contradictory, at least unclear. It is not a self-interpreting story, with study notes at the bottom of each page. Its basic message is far from self-evident, nor is it clear how its prophecies are to be fulfilled, for the material is varied and disparate.

We have the story of the creation of the world, followed quickly by the life of Abraham and God's promise to him that He would give the Land of Canaan to him and his descendants, and that through him all the nations would be blessed. Then come the stories of Isaac and Jacob, and the sojourn in and liberation from Egypt. Then comes the giving of the Law. Then the story of Joshua and the conquest of the Promised Land, then the stories of the Judges, who served God in times of moral apostasy and chaos. Then the establishment of the monarchy, and the covenant with David. Then the long apostasy of Israel, leading to the exile of both the northern and southern kingdoms. Then the words of the Prophets, promising judgment and restoration. And stories of heroism, such as those of Esther and Daniel. And stories of the return of a small remnant to the Land and their struggles there. And as well as this sweeping historical saga, we have psalm and proverb. We even have erotic love poetry.

So, putting it all into an ideological blender and pouring it out as a drink for our souls, what does it all mean? What's the point of it all, and does it all hang together into a coherent whole? Where is all this history, teaching, and poetry leading?

More specifically, does it lead to Judaism, to a religion in which national identity is paramount? Are we to expect the Messiah to be an earthly king of an earthly kingdom, presiding over a *Pax Hebraica*, replacing the *Pax Romana*? Is the rebuilt Temple to serve as the supreme focal point in this kingdom? Is Jerusalem to rule over the world as Rome ruled over the world? Certain passages give that impression. But other passages equally give another and opposite impression. Is the kingdom to be spiritual, consisting in triumph over death, rather than triumph over national enemies? Are physical cultic things like the Ark to be made insignificant? Is the age-old distinction between Jew and Gentile to be obliterated and made irrelevant? In the absence of clear indications and explanations, there is no way to decide between these rival interpretations and other interpretations besides.

The disciples of Jesus, like all other Jews of our Lord's time, could only guess at how the prophecies would be fulfilled. (A favorite hope and guess was that the Kingdom at least involved some kind of national restoration and kicking the Romans out of Palestine.) The Big Picture and how everything fit together was anything but clear—and this was God's intention, for this lack of clarity gave scope for the free will of men, and for the fulfillment of the Scriptures according to plan even by those who didn't know they were doing so (see Acts 13:27).

But the disciples of Jesus knew this at least: that in Jesus, God had come to them in power. His words caused their hearts to burn, and He spoke as no other man had ever spoken—as even His enemies acknowledged (John 7:45–46). He brought joy to the despairing, He forgave sins and gave new life. He opened blind eyes, unstopped deaf ears, cleansed lepers, and even raised the dead. People who met Him felt that He walked the earth with all the authority of God in heaven, and that in meeting Him, they had met this God face to face. The Pharisees and others issued challenges. He didn't keep the Law as they felt pious men should; He ate food without due care for ceremonial cleansing of hands; He had no regard for their understandings of the Sabbath. If He cast out demons, that was only because He was in league with Satan, the prince of the demons.

Then, literally overnight, it was all over. The good people of Jerusalem awoke one Passover Friday and found that by mid-morning the Teacher who they had dared to hope was the Messiah was hanging in disgrace on a Roman cross, His enemies everywhere triumphant.

Then, darkness and an earthquake. Then, a day of rest. And then . . .

Then, another earthquake, and the wide world is still reeling from the aftershocks. The apostles found the Tomb empty. One by one, in early morning meeting and in evening meal, singly and in groups, they found Him alive. For forty days, He appeared and ate and drank with them, and told them how the Law and the Prophets and the Psalms—the whole charter—was fulfilled in Him. The disciples at last came to see how all the details of the Scriptures fit together. Jesus' life and words and ministry, His Cross and Death and Resurrection, were not just the next chapter in Israel's history. They were the fulfillment of that history, the final piece which, when snapped into place, made sense of everything else. Ever since Christ's Cross and Resurrection, Christians have read the Old Testament and found things that before seemed contradictory to be complementary parts of a single coherent whole.

The life of Jesus is the grid we place over the Old Testament texts, the key that interprets and explains everything. Without Christ, the Old Testament remains unclear, its differing passages contradictory, its hopes manifestly unfulfilled. With Christ, we can understand everything. It is as St. Ignatius said so long ago. Our charter is Jesus Christ.

CHAPTER 1

GENESIS: WALKING WITH THE PATRIARCHS

An Overview of Genesis

THE TITLE "GENESIS" IS A TRANSLITERATION of the Greek word for "origin," which might give the impression that one of the main purposes of the book is to relate the story of how the world began. (The Hebrew title of the book conveys no such thematic impression; it is entitled *Bereshith*, from the first two words, "in the beginning." In this it is similar to the title of our Book of Exodus. In Hebrew, that Book is called *Shmoth*, "names," from the opening words, "And these were the names.") We have become so accustomed to the Bible beginning with an account of the creation of the world that we assume such a beginning is inevitable, and that ancient people of course wanted to know how the world began.

In fact, the ancients were singularly uninterested in the cosmic question of how the world began. Most simply assumed its existence, and if they asked themselves any such cosmic questions, they posited that the world had always existed. The creation myths of the pagans functioned very differently from the creation story in Genesis and had no such pride of place in their mythologies. The pagan gods did not style themselves as Creator in the same way as the Jewish God boasted of being the Creator. "The Creation" was not an issue for the ancient world.

Thus, it is not because the question of how the world came to be was a burning one that Genesis opens with the Creation. And the modality or method of creation is not even the main point of the Creation story. The Hebrew creation story was as much polemic as it was anything else. Its main point is not, "This is how the world came into existence," but rather, "Our Jewish tribal God is sovereign over the whole world." What would strike the ancients the most forcefully from the story was not the statement, "God made the world out of nothing," but the statement, "Yahweh Elohim made the world"—and therefore the Hebrews who alone worship this God are assured of victory. In contemporary North America, where proponents of creation science square off against proponents of evolution in a kind of political mud wrestling, and where questions of exactly how the world came into existence dominate the discussion, it is easy to miss the main point of the Creation story. The question of the mechanics of how the world came into existence was not central, or even important. The question of which deity was sovereign was.

The Book of Genesis is mainly about the creation of the Jewish people, and the story of the creation of the world functions as its backdrop. We see this when we step back to observe the large sweep of the narrative. First come stories of the creation of the world and of the human race by the Jewish God, which by implication dethrone all other gods and deny their claims to sovereignty and power. Next come stories of the Fall, the first murder, the growth of cities and civilization, all of which are related with reference to the Jewish God alone. Then comes the story of the destruction of the world by a Flood, and the preservation of a few in the Ark, all by the power of the Jewish God. It is important not to miss the main point of this story: that it was the Jewish God that acted upon the world stage to create and judge and save. He is the One who is offended by man's hubris and pride and the Tower of Babel; He is the One who scatters them in judgment. The other gods are not in the picture.

Thus, the Book of Genesis does not so much narrate the history of mankind as the story of Yahweh Elohim, the Jewish God. That is why the story of the world's history continues without a break with the calling of Abraham and Yahweh's covenant with him. Yahweh acted to create, judge, and save the world in the first eleven chapters. He continued to act in chapters twelve and following by calling Abraham, and creating from him the Jewish people, and giving them the land of Canaan as His gift.

The stories in the early chapters are not answering the question, "So what happened before Abraham in the history of the world?" This was never a burning question. These stories answer the question, "What assurance do we Jews have that we can continue to thrive in the Promised Land when we are surrounded by so many powerful pagan nations?" The answer: "The God we worship is the One who made those pagan nations and who is sovereign over all the earth."

The writer or writers of Genesis make no claim to be writing objective history. No one in those days ever did. Their central claim is more important and more emphatic. In a sea of paganism, surrounded by temples and altars to rival gods whose worshippers seemed to possess all the political power and cultural influence there was to be had in the world, Genesis insisted, "Our God *is* in heaven; He does whatever He pleases" (Ps. 115:3). Genesis, whatever its historical value, was not primarily written for historians in the towers of Academia, but for worshippers of Yahweh on the field of battle.

The Trinity in Genesis

In Genesis 1:26, God (Heb. *Elohim*) refers to Himself in the plural: "Let Us make man in Our image, according to Our likeness." The plural recurs again in Genesis 3:22: "Then the LORD [Heb. *Yahweh*] God said, 'Behold, the man has become like one of Us, to know good and evil.'" And once again in Genesis 11:7: "Come, let Us go down and there confuse their language."

The use of the plural to describe God has not failed to attract Christian exegetical attention throughout the years. Commenting on Genesis 1:26, St. Augustine said, "because [man] is made in the image of the Trinity, consequently it was said, 'in Our image.'" Commenting on Genesis 3:22, St. Ephraim the Syrian wrote, "By saying, 'He has become like one of Us,' [the writer] symbolically reveals the Trinity." These Fathers have had their share of modern counterparts throughout the years who have also suggested the plural as indicating the Trinitarian nature of God.

There is, however, a need for careful nuance as we interpret this passage. The original writer is not advancing an overt Trinitarianism. There is no suggestion that he knew God was three as well as one, and the plural found here is rarely found again outside of these passages in Genesis where God speaks in power and judgment. (Isaiah 6:8 is the only other example: "Whom shall I send, / And who will go for Us?"[1]) The God of Israel is portrayed as a single Person, not a Trinity, for the revelation of the true Trinitarian nature of the Godhead would await the Incarnation of the Son of God. Most likely these plural references are what some have called the "plural of majesty," or the "plural of fullness," and are used to indicate His immense sovereignty. Even in English, the monarch expresses sovereignty by making decrees using the personal plural (as in Queen Victoria's famous, "We are not amused"). We note the same linguistic phenomenon in the Quran, where Allah often speaks in the plural, without any suggestion of a Trinity of Persons.

If the Old Testament were simply human literature, no different from other literature of the ancient Near East, that would be the end of it. But Christians affirm that as well as being human literature, it is also the Word of God, and carries meaning deeper than that intended by its authors (compare 1 Pet. 2:10–12). Thus St. Ephraim said that the Trinity is revealed "symbolically"—or, as we should say, prophetically. The author of Genesis might simply have meant to show the fullness of God's majesty. We Christians know that this fullness subsists in three divine Persons, Father, Son, and Holy Spirit, and we find this Trinitarian fullness hidden in the divine plurals of Genesis.

---

1 Rendered in the Septuagint as "Whom shall I send, and who will go to this people?"—possibly avoiding the plural to avoid the appearance of polytheism. Similar theological concerns are apparent in other renderings. For example, in Ex. 3:6, where the Hebrew reads, "[Moses] was afraid to look upon God," the Septuagint translator rendered it, "[Moses] was afraid to look down before God" (Gr. *katemblepsai enōpion tou theou*)—obviously because the translator did not believe one could see God. A similar change from the Hebrew is found in the Greek rendering of Ex. 24:11, where "they saw God" becomes "they appeared in the place of God."

This later Christian perspective allows us to see even deeper into the historical text and to read it in a Trinitarian way. Obviously, the God of Israel is the Father of our Lord Jesus Christ. It is the Father who was worshipped by Israel in the Old Testament days—the Temple was the House of Yahweh, and Christ says that the Temple is also His Father's House (John 2:16)—thus the Father is that Yahweh who was worshipped in the Old Testament. We affirm this identity of Yahweh with the Father in the Creed when we say, "I believe in one God, the Father Almighty."

But the Father is revealed, manifested, and known only in His Son. Just as a man is known through his mind and word and reason, so the Father is known through His Word, His divine Logos. "No one has seen God at any time. The only begotten Son, who is in the bosom of the Father, He has declared *Him*" (John 1:18). Christ is thus the visible "image of the invisible God" (Col. 1:15). It follows then that all revelations of the Father are through the Son (which is why the Incarnation of God was the Incarnation of the Son, and not of the Father or the Spirit). When God appeared in an Old Testament theophany, it was the divine Logos who appeared, as the revelatory image of the Father. That is why St. John says that Isaiah "saw [Christ's] glory and spoke of Him" (John 12:41). When did Isaiah see Christ's glory? At his vision of the glory of God in the Temple, narrated in Isaiah 6:1ff: "I saw the Lord sitting on a throne, high and lifted up, and the train of His *robe* filled the temple." Isaiah saw the thrice-holy Yahweh of Hosts. Yet St. John says that Isaiah saw Christ, for Yahweh, God the Father, manifests Himself through His divine Logos. The Fathers were not wrong to see all Old Testament theophanies as manifestations of the divine Logos.

This vision continues to be expressed in our Orthodox hymnography as well: Kassia, in her famous hymn sung on the Bridegroom Matins of Holy Week, writes of Jesus, "Once Eve heard Your footsteps in Paradise in the cool of the day." She is referring, of course, to Yahweh's approach to the erring Eve and Adam in the Garden of Eden after their fall, when they heard His footsteps and went and hid themselves (Gen. 3:8). Kassia identifies this Yahweh with Christ, continuing in the biblical tradition that sees the Father, Yahweh, God of Israel, manifesting Himself through His coeternal Son.

Is the Trinity in the Old Testament? Exegetically, no. "Symbolically" (to use St. Ephraim's word), yes. Taught by the New Testament about the unity of the Father and the Son, we can look back into the Old Testament and trace His preincarnate footsteps.

Man and the Destruction of Evil: Genesis 3:15

Famous as the "first preaching of the Gospel" (i.e. the "protoevangelium") is Genesis 3:15, God's word to the serpent after the Fall:

> "And I will put enmity
> Between you and the woman,
> And between your seed and her Seed;
> He shall bruise your head,
> And you shall bruise His heel."

What does this passage mean? It is unlikely that it merely serves as an etiological explanation of man's hatred of snakes: the other divine pronouncements in Genesis 3:16–19 speak of such cosmic and fundamental realities as pain in childbearing, weakness, toil, and death. Whatever the judgment on "the serpent" means, it must involve something more fundamental to human existence than man's proverbial dislike of snakes.

In its primary historical context, the passage refers to the warfare between evil and good. Satan (the serpent is clearly an image for something more momentous than a simple snake) thought to ensnare all of Eve's descendants, but God here declares that they will fight back and eventually prevail. The seed of the serpent refers to those men who choose to rebel against God as the serpent did. The seed of the woman then refers to those men who fight against such evil. (The fight of man against such bestial evil also finds reference in Genesis 4:7: "sin lies at the door" like an animal, "And its desire *is* for you, but you should rule over it.") Here God pronounces final judgment on the serpent, promising that men will eventually destroy the evil that once led them astray.

One knowing only Old Testament realities would understand this simply as a declaration that God's righteousness will finally prevail on earth. But from our vantage point in the Church, we can look back and see exactly how this divine declaration was fulfilled. Christians reading about this final judgment on the serpent inevitably apply it to Christ's destruction of Satan, and see in it a promise of what they experience in Christ. Christ made war against the serpent, healing all who were oppressed by the devil (Acts 10:38), and finally casting Satan down from authority through His Cross (John 12:31; Rev. 12:9). Christ did indeed strike at his head, crushing and destroying his power, though at the cost of Satan striking at His heel as He suffered on the Cross. Man did indeed win the victory over evil through the Man Jesus Christ. The woman's seed or offspring (Heb. *zerah*, which can indicate both the individual and the collective) refers to all men who war against evil, as well as their representative and champion, the Lord Jesus. This text is truly a first preaching of the Gospel.

This text, coming at the opening chapters of the Book of Genesis, reveals that God intended the Incarnation from the beginning and that Christ's sacrifice was "foreordained before the foundation of the world" (1 Pet. 1:20). Such is the immensity of God's love that Adam and Eve had not even been expelled from Paradise for their sin before He promised salvation. Even in the pronouncement of the just sentence of condemnation for their sin, God took care to comfort them with an assurance of eventual victory over the evil that ensnared them.

Noah and Salvation through the Water: Genesis 6—9

The story of Noah and the Ark is about Yahweh's sovereignty over the world. Debates over the historicity of the Flood tend to blind us to the central point of the story, which is that it was the Jewish God who created the world, and then also destroyed it, and then recreated it, so that nations rightly owe their loyalty and worship to Him.

The salvation of the world after the Flood is presented as a second act of creation (especially when read in the original Hebrew). In the first creation, God's *ruach* (Spirit) moved upon the face of the primeval waters of chaos, bringing form out of that chaos and filling the void with living creatures. As St. Peter said, the earth was formed out of water, by means of water (2 Pet. 3:5). In the second re-creation, the *ruach* (or wind) from God again moved over the waters that had brought the chaos of destruction upon the world (Gen. 8:1).

The Hebrew word *ruach*, used in both Genesis 1:2 and 8:1, is usually translated by the different words "spirit" and "wind" in the English versions, which can obscure the intended connection between the two acts of creation. (The same Greek word, *pneuma*, is also used in the Septuagint in both Gen. 1:2 and 8:1.) God shows Himself sovereign over the forces of chaos in both acts of creation.

This unity of creation and re-creation finds expression in the rest of the Old Testament. In Psalm 104, chanted every Vespers, the account of creation is described with the words, "You covered it with the deep as *with* a garment; / The waters stood above the mountains. / At Your rebuke they fled; / At the voice of Your thunder they hastened away" (vv. 6–7). The description fits both the first creation and the second re-creation, when the waters of the Flood subsided and the mountains reappeared (Gen. 8:5). In Psalm 29, the Psalmist declares, "The LORD sat *enthroned* at the Flood, / And the LORD sits as King forever" (v. 10). The Hebrew word translated "flood" is *mabul* (Gr. *kataklusmos*), the same word used in both the Hebrew original and the Greek translation to describe the Flood of Noah. Is this psalm talking about God's sovereignty in the original act of creation, or His re-creation after the Flood? The psalm is ambiguous—and that is the point. There is an abiding unity between the original creation before Adam and the re-creation after Noah.

We assume today (correctly) that there is only one God, and so we miss the polemical content of the original Flood story. When this story was first circulated, Yahweh was only one deity among many worshipped in the ancient Near East. Yet the Flood story asserts that it was Yahweh who was grieved at the world's sin, and that it was a man who pleased Yahweh who was chosen by Him to survive. It was Yahweh who exercised power, not just over His Land of Palestine (His proper "jurisdictional turf" as far as the pagans were concerned), but over the whole earth. He was One who destroyed the world and then recreated it. The first sacrifices offered in the renewed world were offered to Yahweh (Gen. 8:20). The polemical intent is unmistakable.

Christians reading this story of judgment, grace, and covenant

Genesis

mercy read it with different eyes than others, eyes which have been enlightened in baptism. In this story, we read of a world darkened by sin, a world under God's judgment and doomed to destruction. We read of one chosen by God to grant the world rest (in Gen. 5:29 the name "Noah" is paired with the word "rest" [NKJV, "comfort"]). We read of a chosen few, different from the unrighteous world and scorned by them. These chosen ones are surrounded by water, which drowns the old world of sin. We read of Noah and his family coming safely through the waters to live in a new world washed clean of sin, and of their offering sacrifices to God immediately upon entering into this new world.

That is, when we read these words in Genesis, we read there our own story. Christians also live in a world darkened by sin and doomed to destruction (compare 2 Pet. 3:7), an unrighteous world that scorns and persecutes us. We know of the Chosen One, Jesus, who grants rest to the weary (Matt. 11:29). In baptism we are surrounded by water, a water that drowns our old sinful way of life, separating us forever from that past. We come safely through the waters of baptism to live in the Kingdom of God, a new creation. And the first thing we do liturgically after our baptism is to offer, with the faithful, the Sacrifice of the Eucharist. Noah's story is our story. (We find other parallels too, as we dig deeper into the text: The dove of Noah carried in its beak a twig of olive, the sign of new life. In our baptismal chrismation, the Holy Spirit is given through the anointing with olive oil, giving new life. Also, eight people were in the Ark, and eight is the number of resurrection and eternity.)

The story of Noah and the Flood therefore yields prophetic significance when read from within the Church. In seeing in the story both type and antitype, the pattern and fulfillment of our baptism (see 1 Pet. 3:20–21), the Church does not exercise perverse ingenuity, thrusting upon the text something foreign to it. Believing that the Scriptures are prophetic, we cannot help but see there our own experience, and we conclude that such astonishing correspondences cannot be accidental. We are not arbitrarily reading something into the text, but discerning the meaning God has already hidden there for us to find.

In typifying our baptismal salvation under the figures of the Ark and the Flood, the Scriptures challenge us to utterly reject the sin that characterized our old prebaptismal life and continues to characterize the world. When Noah and his family emerged from the Ark into the new world, they were utterly cut off from the old world, with no possibility of returning to it, for that old world had been destroyed. In the same way, St. Paul urges us to consider ourselves as utterly cut off from our old ways. He writes, "our old man was crucified with *Him*, that the body of sin might be done away with, that we should no longer be slaves of sin. . . . reckon yourselves to be dead indeed to sin, but alive to God in Christ Jesus our Lord" (Rom. 6:6, 11). For us, as with Noah, there can be no going back.

The world judges our new way of righteousness to be folly, even as Noah's generation considered his righteousness to be folly. As St. Peter writes, "they think it strange that you do not run with *them* in the same flood of dissipation, speaking evil of *you*" (1 Pet. 4:4). But we must not let their words intimidate us; we must persevere in the new way. The flood proved Noah's folly was wisdom, and the coming last judgment will vindicate us as well.

Abraham and the Blessing of the Nations: Genesis 12:1–3

After the global events of the Creation, the Fall, the Flood, and the scattering of the nations, the narrative spotlight suddenly narrows its focus in chapter 12 to a single family: Terah, his son Abraham, Lot, and those belonging to them. We hear God calling Abraham to leave his people and his land and to live the rest of his life as a visionary wanderer. The succeeding chapters of Genesis (and of all the Pentateuch) will focus on the fortunes of this extended family.

God's call to Abraham to go out from his country and his father's house to the land that He would show him was accompanied by a promise. God promised Abraham,

> "I will make you a great nation;
> I will bless you
> And make your name great;
> And you shall be a blessing.
> I will bless those who bless you,

And I will curse him who curses you;
And in you all the families of the earth shall be blessed."
(Gen. 12:2–3)

We see in this promise the same global scope found in the previous chapters. The narrative may focus on one family, but God's purposes remain cosmic and His concern, universal.

The question remains: How are these purposes to be fulfilled? In what way does Abraham become a blessing to all the families of the earth? Put another way, what is the connection of this grand promise with the subsequent history of Israel?

One possible answer is that the Law fulfills the promise to Abraham, so that the connection of Abraham with Moses is that of prophecy with its fulfillment. This answer asserts that what God was promising Abraham was nothing more than that a nation would be established which looked back to him as its forefather. The promise to Abraham was the preliminary sketch; the Law given to Moses was the completed picture. God's goal in calling Abraham was the establishment of the Jewish State. In this vision, the Law is the summit and pinnacle of God's revelation, the goal of all God's acts among the sons of men. Salvation is national salvation, and the Israelites enjoy a place of privilege. God has nothing grander in His purposes for His world than the exaltation of His chosen nation.

This, of course, is the vision and answer of classical Judaism. But when we try to place this vision within the great sweep of the Genesis narratives, we run into problems. One problem is that it is difficult to see how exalting the nation of Israel over the rest of the nations, so that Israel is the head and the Gentiles the tail (see Deut. 28:13), could conceivably be viewed by any of those nations as their being blessed by Abraham or his descendants. They might view Abraham and his seed as tyrannizing over them or using them, but not as blessing them. The vision of a strictly national fulfillment of the promise to Abraham, whatever its merits in Jewish eyes, utterly fails to fulfill the words of God about blessing all the families of the earth.

Another problem with this national vision is its narrowness. Abraham begot Ishmael as well as Isaac, and Isaac begot Esau as well as Jacob.

One could understand how the purposes of national existence must be fulfilled in Isaac, not Ishmael, and in Jacob, not Esau. It is less easy to understand how that national existence somehow fulfills the glorious promise to Abraham about blessing all the earth. If divine blessing is offered only to the nation of Israel, other nations and tribes are discarded as utterly irrelevant to the divine promise. How could it be that the God who promised to bless all the families of the earth has no use for or interest in any other nation but Israel? The early chapters of Genesis showed Yahweh as God of all the earth—is He now to be considered utterly uninterested in blessing anyone other than the nation of Israel? Such a vision of the fulfillment of the promise to Abraham cannot be squared with the global scope of God's concern in the introductory and foundational chapters.

It is this disjunction between the global focus of God's promise to Abraham on the one hand, and the narrowly nationalistic focus of the Mosaic Law on the other, to which St. Paul calls attention in Galatians 3. God's promise to Abraham to bless all nations was sure and certain; the blessing available to the Israelite nation under the Law was conditional and quite uncertain. (It was often completely forfeited, as Israel's history of apostasy shows.) The promise to Abraham was therefore on quite another plane than the Law of Moses. Israel's Law and national history indeed had their purpose in the overarching providence of God. The Law was not irrelevant to His purposes. Indeed, the Law was God's covenant instrument to teach Israel the lessons it needed to learn, and Israel's long national existence is the abiding record of those lessons. But the Law was not the fulfillment of the Promise. The Promise of global blessing to the nations was to be fulfilled in something else.

Christians, having experienced the grace of Christ, know what that "something else" is. We look at God's promise that through Abraham He will bless all the peoples of the earth. Then we look at the spread of the Gospel and see that it is through Jesus, the son of Abraham, that blessing and life are reaching all the peoples of the earth before our very eyes. It is impossible not to see the latter as the fulfillment of the former. Clearly, the promise to Abraham is ultimately fulfilled not in the Jewish Law and Israel's national existence, but in the Gospel, which gives life to Jew and Gentile alike. Abraham was not simply the forefather of the

Jewish nation. He was the forefather of all who, through conversion to Christ, put their faith in God even as Abraham did. In this way, Abraham indeed became the father of many nations (Gen. 17:5).

The Priest-King Melchizedek: Genesis 14:17–20

The neighbors of Abraham recognized that he was a great man (a mighty sheik, in modern terms), very wealthy, and with what we would call a private army at his command. When a powerful northern coalition carried away his nephew Lot in a raid on local towns, Abraham was able to lead three hundred and eighteen men to pursue and overtake them and return to the locals what the raiders had taken (including his kinsman Lot). The story is told in Genesis 14.

In the midst of the narrative, after Abraham's return from battle, someone comes from out of nowhere (at least as far as the narrative is concerned):

> Then Melchizedek king of Salem brought out bread and wine; he *was* the priest of God Most High. And he blessed him and said:
> "Blessed be Abram of God Most High,
> Possessor of heaven and earth;
> And blessed be God Most High,
> Who has delivered your enemies into your hand."
> And he gave him a tithe of all. (Gen. 14:18–20)

The sudden appearance of Melchizedek is startling, especially when the passage is read with Jewish eyes. Any priest, to function as a priest, needed the correct lineage (in later Mosaic terms, the lineage of Levi and Aaron). But nothing is said of Melchizedek's lineage, or even of his history. He is not introduced. He simply appears. Then, after providing a feast of bread and wine, he blesses Abram, and then vanishes. Not literally, of course. After Abram left, Melchizedek of course returned to Salem, where he ruled as king (kingship was local and limited in those days). But as far as the narrative is concerned, he vanishes into thin air, and we hear nothing more of him. We don't know who his father or mother was, or what happened to him, or when or how he died. In the story he functions (as C. S. Lewis once said[2]) as a *numinus* figure, almost as someone from another world. He certainly was greater than Abram, since Abram gave him a tenth of the spoils.

From what did Melchizedek derive his priesthood? From his kingship. That is, he was able to function as priest for Salem and offer their sacrifices to the local supreme deity, God Most High (Heb. *El Elyon*), because he was the king of Salem. The idea of a king having access to God (and with it, to divinely sent victory) continued to resonate in Israel, and David refers to his royal descendants having this priestly access to God and victory when he wrote that his royal seed would be "a priest forever according to the order of Melchizedek" (Ps. 110:4).

For us Christians, who believe that Jesus was the messianic heir of David, this is extremely important. The Messiah is king by definition, and David's psalm means that Messiah is also a priest—not of the earthly Temple (there were already Levitical priests for that), but the true Temple and dwelling of God in heaven, of which the earthly Temple was the model. Every Sunday, Christians gather with our clergy to offer the eucharistic sacrifice, receiving through the bread and wine the blessing of Jesus, our heavenly Priest-King.

So it is that when we read about Melchizedek, we cannot help but read about our own weekly worship. Chapter 7 of the Epistle to the Hebrews draws out all the prophetic parallels in loving detail. Melchizedek is the king of Salem (by translation, the king of peace), and his very name means "king of righteousness." (Etymological accuracy is unimportant, for Old Testament etymologies are often based more on wordplays than anything else.) In the same way, Jesus is the king of peace and the king of righteousness, since He brings God's peace and righteousness to His people. Melchizedek appears in the text out of nowhere and vanishes in the same way, for the narrative records neither his human lineage nor his death. In the same way, Christ is eternal, having no human father or mother, but eternally coexisting with the Father before His incarnation from the Virgin. And Christ lives forever, no longer being subject to death. What Melchizedek is textually in the

---

[2] In his *Reflections on the Psalms*.

narrative, Christ is actually in history, "having neither beginning of days nor end of life" (Heb. 7:3). Melchizedek is greater than Abraham, even as Christ is greater than Abraham. And Melchizedek feasts Abraham with bread and wine, even as Christ feasts His people with bread and wine at the eucharistic sacrifice. For us Christians, the appearance of the historical priest-king Melchizedek points toward Abraham's descendant, the glorified Priest-King Jesus. Abraham acknowledged Melchizedek by offering a tithe. We acknowledge our Lord Jesus by offering Him our very lives.

Abraham and Faith: Genesis 15 and 17

God appeared to Abraham when he was an old man, and when his wife Sarah was an old woman, well past the time of childbearing. God promised him descendants, but did not immediately fulfill His promise. Waiting proved hard, and Sarah decided to take matters into her own hands. She gave her slave-girl Hagar to her husband, knowing that the child born of the union would be legally Sarah's.

God said He would bless that child (Ishmael by name), but would not fulfill His promise of covenant descendants through him. Rather, God would give elderly Sarah miraculous conception through her union with her husband, despite the old age of both. In the words of God to Abraham in Genesis 15:4, "one who will come from your own body shall be your heir." Abraham believed this promise, "and [God] accounted it to him for righteousness" (v. 6).

Sarah was initially incredulous, but God was determined to give Abraham covenant offspring as the fruit of his union with Sarah: "I will bless her," God said to Abraham, "and also give you a son by her" (Gen. 17:16). Abraham prostrated himself before God and laughed, saying, "Shall *a child* be born to a man who is one hundred years old? And shall Sarah, who is ninety years old, bear *a child*?" (v. 17). As it turns out, the answer was yes.

Since God had called Abraham much earlier, when he was still in Mesopotamia, He could have granted conception at an earlier time, in the years when childbearing was still biologically possible for the couple.

But God waited until such a birth was a biological impossibility in order to show His power, and as a sign that He would fulfill the rest of His promise to multiply the descendants and make them great. God called Abraham to believe the impossible—that He could grant conception to them despite their age—or, to quote St. Paul, despite the fact that Abraham's "body" was "already dead," and despite "the deadness [Gr. *nekrōsis*] of Sarah's womb" (Rom. 4:19). That is, Abraham was asked to have faith that God could bring life out of death.

Once again we see this as foreshadowing our own faith. Abraham's faith was the prototype of our own and set the pattern for it. Abraham had faith in God, and it was reckoned as righteousness, giving him lasting blessing from God. We Christians have faith, and it is reckoned as righteousness to us also. The object of that faith is the same in both cases: life out of death. Abraham believed a living son could emerge from the womb of death; Christians believe the living Son emerged from the tomb of death. The miraculous birth of Isaac foreshadowed his descendant Christ's miraculous Resurrection. Saving faith is faith that God brings life out of death. Such a faith may seem foolish in the world's eyes (how could Abraham and Sarah have a child when they were both so elderly?), but God's actions justify our trust in Him.

The Hospitality of Abraham: Genesis 18

A greatly beloved icon is Rublev's Holy Trinity, a reworking of an icon depicting the Hospitality of Abraham. In Rublev's icon, we see three Persons sitting in perfect unity around a table. In the original icon of the Hospitality of Abraham, we see not only those three Persons, but also Abraham and Sarah, for whom the icon is named. Rublev has omitted all but the Three themselves, to focus on the divine unity of the Three in One. Familiarity with his icon makes it easy to see the Holy Trinity in the story of the hospitality of Abraham and Sarah found in Genesis 18.

What Rublev offers us, however, is typology, not exegesis. A careful exegesis of the passage and its wider context reveals not three divine Persons visiting Abraham, but Yahweh and two accompanying angels. This is apparent from the flow of the narrative. In Genesis 18:1–2 we read, "Then the LORD appeared to [Abraham] by the terebinth trees of Mamre, as he was sitting in the tent door in the heat of the day. So he lifted his eyes and looked, and behold, three men were standing by him." Abraham addressed the leader as "my Lord" (Heb. *adonai*, the usual term of respect, equivalent to the modern "sir").

After enjoying the hospitality of Abraham, "the men rose from there and looked toward Sodom, and Abraham went with them to send them on the way" (v. 16). Yahweh then shared with his friend Abraham His plan to destroy Sodom. Then "the men turned away from there and went toward Sodom, but Abraham still stood before the LORD" (v. 22), to attempt to dissuade Him from destroying Sodom if a few righteous people could be found there. The men, identified in Genesis 19:1 as "the two angels," continued to Sodom to rescue Lot and his family from the inevitable imminent destruction. It is clear from this wider context that the hospitality offered by Abraham to his three supernatural visitors was in fact offered to Yahweh and the two angels sent to destroy Sodom and Gomorrah.

Classical Christian exegesis, reflected in Rublev's famous icon, has always been impressed with the number of Abraham's supernatural visitors. The text says Yahweh visited Abraham, and Abraham looked up and saw three. If Yahweh had come accompanied by one angel, Abraham would have seen two Persons; if He had been accompanied by three angels, the patriarch would have seen four. Those who know that God subsists as Trinity can hardly fail to be struck by the juxtaposition of Yahweh with the number three. The hospitality of Abraham is justly considered as foreshadowing the triple nature of the Godhead, but this typology should not lead to erroneous exegesis. That is, we should not conclude that the three were the Father, Son, and Holy Spirit, each of the divine Persons appearing before Abraham. Such a conclusion would not only defy the larger context, which says that the other two were angels; it would lead to difficult theological problems as well.

As said above (see page 21), the invisible Father who was worshipped in Old Testament times under the Name "Yahweh" always reveals Himself in His dealings with humanity through His Logos. All Old Testament theophanies of Yahweh are in fact manifestations of the preincarnate Son, for the Father always reveals Himself through the Son. If Abraham saw earthly theophanies of all three, the Father, the Son, and the Holy Spirit, it would contradict this basic Christological teaching. There can be no separate theophany of the Father by Himself, a theophany that is not through the Son. And there can be no separate theophany of the Spirit of the Father. The Spirit indeed works among men, strengthening them and inspiring them and giving words to the prophets. But there can be no visible image of the Spirit. That is why He can have no authentic icon or portrait. He was never incarnate and never revealed Himself in theophany as the Father did through His Logos. The Rublev icon illustrates the hospitality to make a typological point.

Abraham and the Binding of Isaac: Genesis 22

Isaac was the embodiment of all God's promises to Abraham. Against hope, Abraham believed God when He promised him a son in his old age, and accordingly, his wife conceived and bore him Isaac. Earlier he had begotten Ishmael through their servant-girl Hagar, and though, according to the customs of that time, Ishmael was legally Sarah's son, yet God was adamant that He would give Abraham a multitude of descendants and a glorious future through Isaac, not Ishmael.

Thus, when God demanded that Abraham offer up Isaac as a human sacrifice (something not unknown in that culture), it seemed as if God were reneging on His promise to give Abraham descendants through Isaac. How could Isaac beget descendants if he were dead? The normal human heartbreak at losing a beloved son was thus compounded by this contradiction when God demanded that Abraham sacrifice Isaac.

The story is related in Genesis 22. Without telling the boy what he plans to do, Abraham takes his son to the designated mountain in the land of Moriah. At the bottom of the hill, he tells his two young servants to wait for them to return (note the plural: the servants were to expect the return of both Abraham and Isaac). He then takes Isaac up to the hilltop to offer the sacrifice. Isaac thinks his father is going to offer the usual animal sacrifice of a lamb. He comments on the presence of the wood and fire and sacrificial knife, but the strange absence of the sacrificial lamb. Abraham simply answers, "God will provide for Himself the lamb" (v. 8).

When they reach their destination, Abraham builds the altar, lays out the wood for the fire, binds his son, lays him on the altar, and goes to get the sacrificial knife to slay him. At the last moment, God calls from heaven and forbids Abraham to hurt the boy, explaining that He needed Abraham to pass the ultimate test of obedience. Now that Abraham has shown himself ready to do anything for God, God reaffirms His promise to him, swearing solemnly that He will multiply his descendants as the stars of heaven. Abraham finds a ram caught in a nearby thicket and sacrifices it instead.

The story is pivotal in classic Jewish piety, which refers to this story as Isaac's Binding (Heb. *akedah*) and makes it the foundation of Israel's merit. Christians also profit by the lesson, learning that faith involves unconditional obedience to God. But Christians see in the story a deeper significance.

It is impossible not to be struck by the convergence in this narrative of so many elements from the life of Christ. Consider the following details: Abraham comes to offer a sacrifice on a mountain in the land of Moriah, a place identified by 2 Chronicles 3:1 with the site of the later Temple—i.e. the approximate site of the sacrifice of Christ on the Cross. The required sacrifice is Isaac, described as the father's "beloved son" (Greek *agapetos*, the same word used in Genesis 22:2 LXX, and in Matt. 3:17 to describe Jesus). Abraham describes the sacrifice with the words, "God will provide for Himself the lamb," even as Jesus was described by John the Baptizer as the Lamb of God (John 1:36). And Abraham apparently expects that after Isaac's sacrificial death, he will rise again so that God's word can be fulfilled, since he says to his waiting servants that both will return (Gen. 22:5).

Given all these parallels with Christ, it is not surprising that we are compelled to see the binding of Isaac as a foreshadowing and prophecy of the death of Christ. When the writer of Hebrews 11:19 says that Abraham received Isaac back from certain death as a *parabolē*, a typological parable, he is only expressing the obvious Christian meaning. Abraham's faith in God on Mount Moriah was typologically tied to his faith in a

God who will later raise from the dead His beloved Son, sacrificed as a lamb on a Jerusalem hilltop.

Jacob, Ephraim, and the Supplanting of the Older Brother: Genesis 25 and 27

In the days of the Patriarchs, one's birth order held great social and legal significance, for the firstborn son possessed tremendous advantages, including rights of property, inheritance, and leadership of the clan after the death of the father. In that social world, the younger always served the elder. It therefore came as a great shock when Isaac and Rebekah were told by God that she was pregnant with twins, and that contrary to all custom and right, the elder would serve the younger. The younger boy, Jacob, grew up with this destiny awaiting him, though of course as a youngster he had no idea how his elder brother Esau's natural right as the firstborn would be overturned.

Many modern readers of the stories of Jacob and Esau have felt a bit sorry for Esau when Jacob persuades his famished and impulsive brother to trade his birthright for a single meal (Gen. 25), and when Jacob deceives his father, blind with age, into bestowing on him (through a kind of irrevocable and verbal "last will and testament") Esau's final blessing as firstborn (Gen. 27). But the original hearers of the story did not so much feel sorrow for Esau as admiration for Jacob, who through cleverness, discipline, and courage, against all odds, entered into his divinely promised destiny.

We see the same overturning of the rights of the older brother in favor of the younger in the story of the blessing of Joseph's children, Ephraim and Manasseh, related in Genesis 48. Joseph brought the boys to his father Israel so that he could bless them, putting the elder brother Manasseh in front of Israel's right hand (so he could lay his right hand upon him) and the younger brother Ephraim before Israel's left hand (so he could lay his left hand upon him). Once again, birth order possessed significance: the right hand of honor, bestowing the greater blessing, was reserved for the elder brother Manasseh.

Israel, however, led by God, "stretched out his right hand and laid it upon the head of Ephraim, who was the younger, and his left hand upon the head of Manasseh, crossing his hands, for Manasseh was the firstborn" (Gen. 48:14 NASB). Joseph was dismayed at this overturning of immemorial custom and tried to move his father's hands, so that the right hand lay upon the elder brother. Israel refused, saying, "[Manasseh's] younger brother shall be greater than he" (v. 19). Once again, the elder took second place to the younger.

These stories were important to the early Christian movement as they strove to justify their existence before a hostile Jewish and pagan world. Unlike our culture, in which the advertiser's words "new and improved" are virtually synonymous, the culture of the ancient world did not think newness bestowed advantage. Indeed, it was antiquity that bestowed authenticity, so that a new movement lacked credibility by virtue of its newness. Truth was eternal, so how could a new Faith be true? (It was this feeling that led both Jewish and Christian apologists to insist that whatever was true in ancient Greek philosophy found its origin in the even more ancient Law of Moses.) The Jews had many objections to the Christians in their midst, not the least of which was the novelty of their Faith. How could the Christians assert that the older Jewish faith was supplanted in favor of the younger Christian movement?

Reading these stories of Jacob supplanting the elder Esau and Ephraim supplanting the elder Manasseh provided the Christians with a needed retort. Some might think it outrageous that a new and young Faith could inherit the honor due to the old—but if God could overturn the established order and bless Jacob over Esau and Ephraim over Manasseh, then He could also bless the Church over Judaism. The old Scriptures once again contained the Faith, practice, and destiny of the Church. In the case of the blessing of Ephraim over Manasseh, Christians also were impressed that it was accompanied by the sign of the cross, for Israel crossed his hands when bestowing the blessing of the elder upon the younger. It is clear the Cross was central to this replacement of the elder by the younger and of Judaism by Christianity. As the Orthodox hymn says, "Through Christ's lifting up on the Cross, the Hebrew race has perished" (i.e. lost its preeminence). By rejecting Christ and consigning Him to the Cross, the Jews forfeited their ancestral privilege. Now, the younger Christian movement would inherit their honor.

Jacob and the Ladder of Heaven: Genesis 28

In Genesis 28, Jacob left home and security, fleeing from certain death at the hands of his brother Esau, to seek life and fortune elsewhere. In distress, he went to Paddan-aram, to his uncle Laban. On his way, he stopped to sleep in the outskirts of Luz, where he had a dream. In his dream, he saw a ladder set on the earth with its top reaching to heaven, with the angels of God ascending and descending on it. God appeared to Jacob and renewed the covenant He had made with his fathers Abraham and Isaac, promising He would bring Jacob back safely to his ancestral land.

Prior to having the dream, Jacob was by no means sure of this. As he left home with anxious heart, for all he knew he would die on the road and never see his home and family again. By this dream God assured him he would indeed return in safety and inherit the covenant God made with Abraham and Isaac. Thus it was not Esau, the elder, whom God had chosen as the heir of the covenant (as custom would have expected), but Jacob, the younger. Thereafter, Jacob considered himself as dedicated to the God of his fathers.

The "ladder," of course, was a stairway, not a stepladder (since angels were simultaneously ascending on it to report to God and descending on it to carry out their missions). Having awoken, Jacob declared the place where he lay to be the House of God (Heb. *Beth-el*), a shrine where one could find God, a meeting place between God and men. The dream revealed Palestine as a Holy Land, a locus of theophany, the land where God could be expected to reveal Himself and where men could find access to His saving presence. It foreshadowed God's later presence there through Ark and Temple.

We Christians read about this ladder not only here in Genesis, but also in the Gospels. When Christ first meets Nathanael, He says to him, "Most assuredly, I say to you, hereafter you shall see heaven open, and the angels of God ascending and descending upon the Son of Man" (John 1:51). Neither Nathanael nor any Jew could miss the scriptural reference to Jacob's ladder, on which angels ascended and descended.

Jesus was saying He was Jacob's Ladder, the true *Beth-el*, the true Temple, the place where men could meet God.

Jacob's ladder (or stairway) is but the first of many Old Testament images that describe God's desire to rendezvous with His creation. The Ark, the pillar of cloud, the Temple, all speak of His abiding commitment not just to thunder at men from a safe distance, but to come down and enter into intimate communication and communion with them. This desire and commitment was later fulfilled in the Incarnation. Jacob's ladder is the first of many intimations that God was intent on drawing near.

We Christians, who have experienced the Father's presence in Christ (John 14:9) and have rejoiced that Christ came down from heaven and appeared in the flesh, can benefit by this story of Jacob. Jacob left home in distress, fleeing the wrath of his brother, utterly uncertain of his future. But God, appearing atop the ladder, reassured him that all would be well and that he would inherit his glorious destiny. In the strength of this word, Jacob continued onward to Haran to seek God's will in the years to come, undaunted by the many challenges that faced him and the sufferings he endured (see Gen. 31:38–42). Christians also have many challenges to face, and many sufferings to endure (2 Tim. 3:12). But we can face them with confidence because of our encounter with Jacob's Ladder, the Lord Jesus. He has promised us a glorious destiny as well, and has said that He would never forsake us throughout our life, even as He promised never to forsake Jacob in his sojourning.

Joseph and the Providence of God: Genesis 37—50

The epic story of Joseph forms the culmination of Genesis, bringing the sweeping narrative from its beginning in eternity to its conclusion in a coffin in Egypt. It is the story of a young man, Joseph, a man destined by God for greatness (he dreams that the sun, moon, and stars bow down before him), the son greatly favored by his father. His brothers become jealous of him and conspire to betray him to death, throwing him into a pit. At the last minute, they change their plan and sell him to passing foreign traders, the Ishmaelites, who in turn sell him as a slave in Egypt.

There he is further persecuted for the sake of his righteousness, when he refuses to sleep with his master's wife as she demands. He is falsely accused by her and cast into prison.

But God is with him, and through His supernatural power gives Joseph wisdom to interpret dreams. This power eventually brings him before Pharaoh, who is impressed with such power and exalts Joseph as his second in command, with authority over all the land of Egypt. In this position he puts into effect a plan to store up food, allowing Egypt and all its dependent peoples to survive the coming years of famine. At length Joseph is revealed to his brothers, and they see all the glory God has bestowed on him. They are reconciled to him and enter Egypt at his invitation. The story is one of the great emotional dramas in all literature, told with consummate skill.

If one did not know the story of Jesus, the story of Joseph would be a great dramatic adventure tale and little more. But when Christians read the story of Joseph, we cannot help but see the story of Jesus traced with prophetic lines under the ancient Egyptian sun. Like Joseph, Jesus was destined by God to be exalted over all. Like Joseph, Jesus was the beloved Son of His Father. Like Joseph, Jesus' Jewish kinsmen were jealous of Him and delivered Him into foreign hands, plotting His death. Like Joseph, Jesus was falsely accused and punished for crimes of which He was innocent. Like Joseph, Jesus was taken by God from the depths to the heights, ascending not merely from prison cell to Egyptian throne, but from the grave to the throne of God. Like Joseph, Jesus was at length revealed by God in His glory to His Jewish kinsmen—as St. Peter said to the crowd on Pentecost, "God has made this Jesus, whom you crucified, both Lord and Christ" (Acts 2:36).

The tale of Joseph is the tale of how God in His Providence uses human evil to bless the world. The evil the brothers committed when they plotted Joseph's death led to the family's deliverance from famine. As Joseph himself said to his brothers, "But as for you, you meant evil against me; *but* God meant it for good, in order to bring it about as *it is* this day, to save many people alive" (Gen. 50:20). Joseph's brothers worked betrayal, lies, murder, and evil. But God reversed Joseph's fortunes, using that evil to exalt him to a place of glory, authority, and power from which he could preserve life. Thus, though the brothers did not intend it, their evil produced good; the plotted murder of one man produced life for all. This is not just the story of Joseph's betrayal and exaltation; it is the story of the Cross of Christ and His exaltation to the right hand of God.

The story of Joseph therefore abides as a *typos*, a type, a foreshadowing of the story of Jesus. It is not simply that the stories are eerily similar in pattern and detail. Christians believe the Hebrew Scriptures are prophetic. The God of the future Kingdom is the same God who spoke through the Scriptures in the past, and He gives intimations of His future Kingdom in those Scriptures. Joseph is not the only example of rejection, tribulation, and subsequent exaltation, but the first of many (Moses being another significant one). Like a repeated musical theme in a symphony, this pattern is heard again and again. Christ's rejection, suffering, and subsequent exaltation sum up and recapitulate all the sacred Hebrew history that went before Him. The divine reversal of fortune that took Christ from the Cross to the throne is not a strange exception, an unexpected anomaly in the history of Israel. There should be no reason to stumble over the notion of a Christ crucified (compare 1 Cor. 1:23). It is the way God has always accomplished the salvation of men.

Jacob and the Blessing of His Sons: Genesis 49

As Jacob neared his end, he gathered his sons to him so he could bless them. Because he expected his blessing to be effective, the blessing had prophetic significance as well. In the words of Genesis 49:1, he said to them, "Gather together, that I may tell you what shall befall you in the last days." He spoke to each one of them, beginning with the firstborn, Reuben. Of particular interest to the disciples of Jesus was his blessing of Judah, our Lord's forefather according to the flesh.

When Jacob blessed Judah, he said,

"Judah *is* a lion's whelp;
From the prey, my son, you have gone up.
He bows down, he lies down as a lion;
And as a lion, who shall rouse him?

The scepter shall not depart from Judah,
Nor a lawgiver from between his feet,
Until Shiloh comes;
And to Him *shall be* the obedience of the people.
Binding his donkey to the vine,
And his donkey's colt to the choice vine,
He washed his garments in wine,
And his clothes in the blood of grapes." (vv. 9–11)

The blessing on Judah is lengthy, exceeded only by the blessing on Joseph. It begins with a play on words, the name "Judah" being cognate with the word for "praise" (compare Gen. 29:35). The tribe will be powerful, subjugating their foes. Jacob compares Judah to a lion, so fearsome that none dare rouse him when he lies down to sleep. The tribe's preeminence, symbolized by a ruler's scepter, is assured and firmly established, for the scepter shall never depart from Judah's possession. Jacob envisions an unfailing supply of rulers, each one coming in turn to claim the scepter that belongs to him (v. 10). The tribe will know great prosperity—vines will be so plentiful they will be used to tether donkeys, despite the donkey eating the grapes of the vine to which it is tethered. Indeed, wine will be in such abundance it will be used as scrub water for washing clothes. The blessing portrays a tribe powerful, secure, and prosperous.

The fulfillment of these glowing words lay with the rise of the tribe of Judah under King David and King Solomon, for then the tribe rose to preeminence in Israel, producing a secure line of rulers and enjoying unprecedented prosperity. But as we read this story from within the shadow of the Cross of Jesus, the Lion of the tribe of Judah (Rev. 5:5), we see other things in this prophecy as well.

We look to Jesus, reclining and sleeping in the grave on the first Holy Friday, and see in the lion's sleep an image of His death. We look to Him sitting at the right hand of God, and see in the ruler's scepter an image of His triumphant rule. We look to Him, humble and mounted on a donkey entering Jerusalem, and see in the binding of the foal to the vine and the washing of garments in the blood of the grape an image of His own triumphal entry into Jerusalem on a donkey and the washing of His garments in the blood of the Cross. Jacob's blessing of Judah did not predict these events in the life of his distant descendant, Christ. But the coincidence of poetic metaphor with literal fulfillment is too striking for us to ignore.

These images of power and wealth which are foreseen for Judah's descendants and which find ultimate fulfillment in Jesus are given for our encouragement. The foes the Lion mightily subjugates are *our* foes—the foes of sin, guilt, and death, "the last enemy" (1 Cor. 15:26). The wealth and abundance the Descendant of Judah possesses are given to *us*—the riches of God's kindness, which He will bestow upon us in the ages to come (Eph. 2:7). In reading about the splendor of the tribe of Judah, we look not merely to earthly fulfillment in the days of David and Solomon, but to the final fulfillment in Christ in the age to come. The prosperity and security of this predestined tribe becomes the prosperity and security of all the people of God in Christ Jesus.

God's Work among the Patriarchs

God walked with the Patriarchs, choosing Abraham when he was still far from his destiny, living in Mesopotamia. God miraculously gave him an heir and continued to walk with Abraham's son Isaac and with his grandson Israel, and with Israel's twelve sons and the whole extended family. His providence brought them into Egypt, where they would sojourn for many long years (see Gen. 15:13–16) until His mighty hand would bring them out. God's work with the Patriarchs was a limited one, a small family affair. No one watching Abraham's clan and his immediate descendants could guess that through them He would create a numerous people, and through that people work openly on the stage of the world. During these years, from the call of Abraham to the entry of his descendants into Egypt, God worked quietly, far from the glare of international history and the stare of kings. It was only later, through Moses, that He would burst upon the world scene with terror and glory that would shake the superpowers down to their foundations.

CHAPTER 2

THE LAW: WORSHIPPING WITHIN THE TENTS

An Overview of the Law

THE LAW OF MOSES, though usually thought of as the first five books (the "Pentateuch"), actually does not begin until the Book of Exodus. That Book opens with the story of Moses, the deliverance of Israel from Egypt and their journey through the desert to Mount Sinai, where God meets them and gives them His Law. The Pentateuchal Books of Exodus, Leviticus, Numbers, and Deuteronomy form one continuous narrative. In this narrative, God brings His people from Egyptian bondage to the border of their new life in the Promised Land.

Along the way, He teaches them both by precept and by power. For example, God not only teaches them by precept that He will bestow health and blessing on the nation if they obey Him, but also demonstrates this through His powerful miracles, when He transforms the poisonous waters of Marah into drinkable waters, thus showing them that He is their source of life and healing (Ex. 15). He not only teaches them by precept to keep the Sabbath, but also teaches them by miraculous example, giving them manna from heaven six days a week, with a two-day supply on the sixth day so that they might rest from gathering it on the seventh, Sabbath day (Ex. 16). Thus historical narrative is mingled with legislation, since God uses both to teach His people the Law, the essence of which is that they must love Him with all their heart and serve Him alone, forsaking all other gods and cleaving only to Him.

This legislation forms the basis of their national life. God had promised to bring the descendants of Abraham into the land of Canaan and make them into a great nation. Their national life was to be the stage on which the Creator worked in the world, forming and teaching a people His ways so they would one day be ready to receive His Son in the flesh. They left Egypt a nation of slaves, bound not only to Pharaoh, but also to their passions, and looking to any gods that could help them. Idolatry was bound up within their hearts, since they shared the fallen human nature common to all men. The Law was given as a tutor, an educative tool, to wean them off of their dependence on other gods and to teach them that help and salvation lay within the one true God alone. They needed to learn the lesson that divine blessing depended not only on their external observance of the sacrificial cult, but also on having a pure and faithful heart. Humanity had strayed far from God, and these lessons, basic as they may seem to us now, were difficult ones to learn. God used the Law to create the nation so that His people might slowly learn these lessons.

The Law, therefore, was not the final goal of God's dealing with humanity or with Israel. Its very provisions declare its transitory nature. For example, the Law presupposes a certain level of population, one small enough so that all males could gather three times a year at the central sacred sanctuary (Ex. 23:14). It presupposes a culturally primitive agrarian community, wherein an ox gores a neighbor to death (Ex. 22:28f). These provisions are not such as could apply to all cultures at all times, nor were they meant to. They were not given as God's final word to Israel. His final Word to Israel was to be the Incarnation of the Son of God and the creation of His Church. As St. Paul was later to say, the Law was simply one phase along the way to that goal, a tutor to bring Israel to Christ (Gal. 3:24).

Moses and the Burning Bush: Exodus 3

At first sight, Moses was an unlikely candidate for the role of divine deliverer. Though raised in the privilege of Pharaoh's court in Egypt, he came to side with his ancestral people and killed an Egyptian who was beating an Israelite. The deed became known and created enough complications for Moses that he decided to flee Egypt in order to save himself. He turned his back forever on his Egyptian past and settled down in the land of Midian to raise a family as part of a local clan. In addition to this questionable background, he was not rhetorically eloquent—surely a disqualification for anyone who aspired to negotiate with Pharaoh and secure the release of the nation of Israel from their Egyptian overlords.

God, however, saw things differently and called Moses from the security of his new life. The call came through the sight of a miraculously burning bush, which was aflame with the presence of God and yet was not consumed. God called Moses from out of the bush, identifying Himself as the God of Abraham, Isaac, and Jacob, and telling Moses He was about to deliver Israel from their bondage and bring them to the land He had promised them. And Moses was the one chosen to make this happen. Moses asked that God tell him His Name—a request not just for a verbal identifier, but for an indication of the power with which God would act on behalf of His people. God replied, "I AM WHO I AM." And He said, "Thus you shall say to the children of Israel, 'I AM has sent me to you'" (Ex. 3:14). (The Name "I Am" is from the Hebrew verb "to be," *hayah*, cognate with the Name "Yahweh.")

God thus revealed Himself to Moses as supremely sovereign, as Yahweh, the One whose actions were dictated, hindered, and conditioned by no one, the One powerful enough to deliver His people. He revealed Himself in a bush that burned and yet was not consumed, because the goal of Israel's deliverance was that He might dwell among them, a consuming fire in the midst of a sinful people. The theophany of the burning bush prefigured God's dwelling in the midst of Israel through the Mosaic cultus of the Ark and Tabernacle.

We who experience the presence and power of Jesus Christ know that a further, more perfect fulfillment of the theophany of the burning bush is possible. The experience of the new glory of Jesus leads us to see the former Old Testament glory with different eyes. In the words of St. Paul, "For even what was made glorious had no glory in this respect, because of the glory that excels" (2 Cor. 3:10). Compared to the darkness of paganism, the Law of Yahweh was a light to the world, and His presence through the Ark and the Tabernacle, a unique gift. But the greater light of Christ and the gift of His presence within the Church compels us to reevaluate the former realities of the Old Testament.

In that reevaluation we discern the mixed nature of God's presence among His people in the Old Testament. God had drawn near to them but still remained separated from them. He lived in their midst, but approach to Him was strictly regulated and limited. The vision of God's union with His people, glimpsed at the burning bush, was clearly capable of a greater fulfillment than could be experienced through the Old Testament cultus.

We see this separation of God from His people throughout the Mosaic legislation. For example, neither priest nor worshipper could approach God in sacrifice while ceremonially unclean. Lepers, or anyone who touched a dead body, or one with a menstrual flow, or one with a seminal emission were all alike ceremonially unclean and could not approach God. Moreover, sacrifices could only be offered through the chosen Levitical priests and in the chosen place (i.e. before the Ark), and then only in the way stipulated by God in His Law. The Ark could not be approached by the common worshipper, or even touched. Even the High Priest did not have untrammeled access.

All of these rules served to regulate and limit man's approach to God, which was anything but free and open. Even at Mount Sinai, when God first came down to reveal Himself to Israel, the mountain was cordoned off and the people were forbidden to approach. Indeed, anyone who did dare to approach or even touch the mountain on which God was to descend was to be put to death—and this ban even extended to animals (Ex. 19:12-15). God was approaching, but His people still had to keep away and cleanse themselves through ritual washing and sexual abstinence. The Mosaic cultic regulations thus served to separate Israel from God, keeping them at a safe distance. As the writer to the Epistle of the Hebrews would later write, "the Holy Spirit indicating this, that the way into the Holiest of All was not yet made manifest while the first tabernacle was still standing. It *was* symbolic for the present time" (Heb. 9:8-9).

We Christians recognize that the divine Fire of the burning bush revealed Himself through Jesus of Nazareth. He was one with the Father, the perfect expression of the Father, the great I Am who revealed Himself to Moses. Jesus Himself confessed this when He said, "Before Abraham was, I AM" (John 8:58). This is plain in every Orthodox icon of Christ, for His halo is adorned with the Greek letters o ὡν, *ho on* —"the Being"— the Septuagint Greek translation of the words "I Am" with which God revealed Himself to Moses at the burning bush.

The burning bush therefore not only prefigures the Old Testament cultus, but also functions as a prophecy of the Incarnation, for in Christ we see a fuller and more complete union of God with His people. God could have redeemed His people from afar, sending messages from heaven, or drawing somewhat near but keeping them safely at arm's length. He chose otherwise, desiring to close the gap between heaven and earth and dwelling in the midst of His people despite their sin, rubbing shoulders with them, allowing them to touch Him, to share His food, His life. Through Christ, God came fully into their midst and became fully approachable. It was only through Christ that sinners and lepers and those ceremonially unclean could freely draw near and receive forgiveness, cleansing, and healing (compare Luke 5:12f; 7:36f; 8:43f). Through Christ, the way into the heavenly sanctuary of God's presence was finally opened to His people. Through Him we are one with the divine fire, and yet we are not consumed. The burning bush Moses saw encourages us to pray that the divine Fire may burn ever more brightly in us as well.

Moses and the Staff of God: Exodus 4—14

When Moses first encountered God at the burning bush, he was holding his shepherd's staff. It is important to see that the staff was not a special sign of authority or power (despite its later use as immortalized by Charlton Heston in the film, *The Ten Commandments*). It was the staff all shepherds carried as part of their daily life (compare Ps. 23:4). Yet, despite its workaday character, it became an instrument of power through the Word of God. When Moses protested he was unable to fulfill God's call to liberate Israel from Egypt, God asked him, "What *is* that in your hand?" When Moses answered, "A rod," God bade him cast it on the ground, whereupon it became a snake. Then, when Moses in obedience to God took the snake by its tail, it became a harmless rod again (Ex. 4:1–5). By this God showed Moses that He possessed the power of death and life, and that He would exercise this power through Moses—even though Moses felt himself to be as humble and common as a shepherd's staff.

The subsequent history of Moses in the Book of Exodus reveals God as true to His promise. Moses carried the staff with him into Egypt. With it, Aaron struck the Nile by God's command and turned its waters to blood. At God's command, Aaron held out Moses' staff over Egypt's rivers, canals, and pools so that frogs emerged from them and swarmed over the land. By God's command, he struck the dust of the earth with the staff, and the dust became gnats throughout the land. Moses stretched forth this staff to heaven, and God sent thunder and hail and fire to the earth. Moses stretched out the staff, and God brought locusts with the east wind, devouring all the fruit of the land. And it was with this staff that Moses divided the waters of the Red Sea, bringing death to the Egyptians and life for Israel. It was simply a staff of wood, as humble as any other shepherd's stick, but through the Word of God it became powerful, saving, and life-giving.

This message is of abiding significance, for it is a message that God's power is perfected through weakness. Just as a humble staff became an instrument that could deal out death and life through the Word of God, so Israel, few in number and powerless among the great nations, could become mighty and victorious through that same Word. The humble Moses with his simple staff was the abiding proof of the power of humility before God.

This message of the power of humility is also the message of the Cross, which we Christians recognize. The wood of Moses' staff prefigured the wood of the Cross—and not just because both were wooden. The Cross was a sign of weakness and of powerless humility before the great powers of the earth. Yet through the might of God, this wood also became mighty and victorious, bringing defeat to God's demonic enemies and life and deliverance for those who trusted its power.

We who trust its power, however, must take care to walk in the ways of humility. Christ was content to be powerless in this age and to die on the Cross. In so doing, "[He left] us an example, that you should follow His steps" (1 Pet. 2:21). It is not only that we should be willing to die for the will of God, but also that we should not insist on our own way, nor upon being vindicated in this present age. Sometimes we will be treated harshly and unjustly. When this happens, we must not revile in return or insist that our righteousness be acknowledged. God will vindicate us soon enough. But if we "do good and suffer, if you take it patiently, this *is* commendable before God" (1 Pet. 2:20). We must imitate Christ on the Cross of humility, who "committed *Himself* to Him who judges righteously" (v. 23). Only in this way can we walk in the way of the saving wood.

Pascha and the Saving Sacrificial Lamb: Exodus 12

The judgments of God on Egypt culminated in the death of the firstborn, in the night when Yahweh passed through the land of Egypt on a mission of death. According to His promise to Moses, He would pass over the homes of the Israelites, on the lintels of whose doors He saw the blood of the prescribed sacrificed lamb (Ex. 12). The feast was forever after called "Passover"—in Hebrew *Pesach*, and in Greek *Pascha*, in memory of His passing over their homes and sparing them the judgment of death that fell upon the unprotected homes of the Egyptians. Every year at that time, Israel was commanded to slay the Passover Lamb and eat it, remembering that night of terror and vigil, and the following morning of deliverance and freedom. For it was after this final stroke fell upon Pharaoh and all his land that he relented and drove the Israelites out, allowing them to leave Egypt forever and inherit the promise of freedom in a new land.

Compared to the other feasts kept by the people of Israel, such as the feast of Weeks (or Pentecost), or the feast of Booths, the feast of Passover had special significance. This was the feast of joy *par excellence*, the commemoration of the beginning of their nationhood, their own

Independence Day. In the days of occupation, when they were ruled by the Romans, they kept the Passover looking forward to the days of the Messiah, the future deliverance when they would eat the Passover in perfect freedom. The Passover was their feast of redemption, the day they passed over from slavery to freedom, from sorrow to joy, from Egyptian hopelessness to being heirs of the Promised Land. So definitively did Passover mark the soul of a Jew that it was said every Jew must regard himself as present at the first Passover deliverance.

It was during the paschal days of feasting that Christ was arrested and crucified. According to the Synoptic Gospels, the Last Supper was a Passover meal (compare Luke 22:7–16). This fact alone assured that we would read the original Egyptian Passover as a type and prophecy of the death of Christ. As the apostle cried, "Christ our paschal lamb has been sacrificed!" (1 Cor. 5:7 RSV).

The parallels indeed are striking. Even as the paschal lambs were once slain in Egypt, so Christ also was slain at this paschal season. The paschal blood of the lambs saved the Israelites from the death that befell the firstborn, and the shed blood of Jesus, the Lamb of God, saves us from eternal death. The Passover led Israel from bondage to Pharaoh to freedom in Canaan, and the paschal Sacrifice of Christ leads His disciples from bondage to sin and death, to freedom and life in the Kingdom. The Passover marked the consolidation of the nation of Israel, binding them in covenant to God, and Christ's paschal self-offering binds His disciples together as a holy nation, His own people (1 Pet. 2:9). With the paschal sacrifice of the lambs, we come to the heart of both Mosaic and Christian religion. For both the Israelites of old and the Christians of today, Pascha is salvation.

Salvation through the Red Sea Waters: Exodus 14

The Passover deliverance began Israel's departure from the bondage and misery of their old life. That departure reached its climax by the Red Sea (or the Reed Sea, Hebrew *Yam Suph*). God's power over the waters of the Red Sea recalls His power at the first creation, as well as the re-creation at the Flood. At the Creation, God's *ruach* moved over the waters (Gen. 1:2), and His *ruach* again moved over the waters of the Flood (Gen. 8:1). We see His *ruach* once more moving over the waters in Exodus 14:21, driving back the sea so that Israel could pass through on dry ground.

These three stories are meant to be seen as a continuous series of God's powerful and saving acts. In all three stories—the original Creation, the Flood, and the salvation at the Red Sea—the waters are a symbol of the universal and primeval chaos over which Yahweh shows Himself Master. God's demonstrations of power at the Creation and the Flood were cosmic acts, and by placing the Red Sea deliverance into this context, the narrative gives that event a cosmic significance as well, for the nation of Israel was the stage on which God would act to save the world. Israel was not just one nation among many; it was in the special care of Yahweh, and its deliverance was the supreme manifestation of Yahweh's might among the nations. Yahweh had humbled Egypt, the superpower of its time, thereby revealing Himself as sovereign over the world. It was not surprising that the nation which was His special object of care was to have global importance.

Moreover, not only was this salvation by the Red Sea of cosmic significance (like the Creation and Flood), it was also a new act of creation. The world was created through water by God's creative *ruach*; it was recreated after the Flood by His *ruach* coming upon the waters, and now through water, by His creative *ruach,* the nation of Israel was created.

The parallel between the creation of the world and this new creation of Israel is evident in comparing the two creations. In Genesis 1 we read ten times "God said," as He created by His Word; in Exodus 20, God gave ten words (in Hebrew, *dabarim*). The day of the Exodus marked Israel's rebirth as a people, so that the waters were also the waters of regeneration. Behind them lay their old life of bondage and the forces of destruction and death, the pursuing Egyptian army. Israel passed through the waters and entered into a new life of freedom, leaving behind their old bondage and their defeated enemies. When they emerged from the waters, their old life was utterly gone, and their foes could hurt them no more. Now they belonged to God and lived only to serve and glorify Him, fulfilling His Word, which would be given them as a gift on Mount

Sinai. Nationally speaking, the whole people was born again when they emerged from the waters over which God's *ruach* had come.

Discerning the saving nature of the Red Sea waters leads our exegesis to find in the narrative the waters of our own baptism as well. Israel experienced baptism even as we Christians do. St. Paul, for example, declared that in the Red Sea the Israelites were "baptized into Moses," even as Christians were baptized into Christ (1 Cor. 10:1f). The typology was all the more compelling in that the Israelites experienced other realities that also had their Christian parallels. The Israelites experienced the fiery light of God's presence in the pillar of cloud and fire, an image of the illumining fire of the Holy Spirit the Christians received in baptism.

Also, after their Red Sea experience, the Israelites "ate the same spiritual food" as the Christians and "drank the same spiritual drink" (v. 4). During the Israelites' "postbaptismal" wanderings in the desert, they ate manna, the bread from heaven, and drank water supernaturally provided from the rock, images of the food and drink consumed by Christians in their postbaptismal Eucharists. The first Passover involved the sacrifice of a lamb and salvation through its blood; a baptism in water that led to new life; supernatural food and drink; and the gift of God's Word. These were the very same realities offered the Christians in their paschal baptism. No wonder we see the Red Sea salvation as a prophecy of our own.

In reading the story of Israel's baptism into Moses, we are challenged to take courage. The Israelites cried out in fear when they saw the Egyptian army bearing down upon them, and immediately concluded that Moses had brought them thus far in vain: "Because *there were* no graves in Egypt, have you taken us away to die in the wilderness?" (Ex. 14:11). Though they had seen God's mighty hand in the plagues on Egypt and the death of the firstborn, they were quick to abandon faith in God. We Christians have also seen the mighty acts of Christ and read of His miracles, and He has promised that He will never forsake us (Heb. 13:5). When we feel disaster impending or are tempted to doubt God's provision, we must let the Red Sea baptism recall us to courage and to faith in God. God said to Moses, "Tell the children of Israel to go forward" (Ex. 14:15). We can go forward also, trusting in His care.

The Waters of Death and the Saving Tree: Exodus 15:22-26

After the liberation from Egypt, Israel began the trek through the desolate and deadly Sinai to the mountain which God had designated as His *rendezvous* with His newly redeemed people. After journeying for three days and finding no water, they were in desperate straits. At last they came to a place later called *Marah* (Heb. for "bitterness") which had water, but they found to their anguish that the water was undrinkable. If drunk, it would bring disease and death.

Moses cried to Yahweh for help, and in response, "the Lord showed him a tree" (Ex. 15:25). Moses cast the tree into the water, and the water became sweet—wholesome and drinkable, no longer a source of disease and death, but of life. The object lesson brought a positive precept from God: "If you diligently heed the voice of the Lord your God and do what is right in His sight, give ear to His commandments and keep all His statutes, I will put none of the diseases on you which I have brought on the Egyptians. For I *am* the Lord who heals you" (vv. 25-26). The lesson was unmistakable—as God saved them from disease at Marah because they looked to Him for help, so He would save their nation from plague in the future if they would keep His Law. The lesson is all the clearer in the Hebrew, for when the text says, "the Lord showed him a tree," the word for "showed" is the Hebrew *yarah*, cognate with the word for "Law" (Heb. *torah*).

Just as we discerned the earth-changing power of the Cross in Moses' humble wooden staff, so we here discern the life-giving power of the Cross in the tree cast into the waters of death. The prophetic typology was an obvious one, since Christ was crucified on the tree of the Cross. And the two trees accomplished the same thing: As the tree of Moses turned a source of certain death into longed-for life, so the Cross of Jesus also transformed death into life. The waters of the oasis of Marah, though promising life, yielded only death. Through the power of the tree, that death was transformed. Presumably God could have chosen any desert object as the instrument of healing. The choice of a tree was prophetic and providential, and it pointed to the tree of the Cross. Human existence in this age, like the oasis of Marah, may promise life and fulfillment, but it leads only to death. Like the children of Israel, we may be tempted by our sorrows in this "vale of tears" to deny God's goodness and embrace despair. Then is the time to remember that through the power of the Cross, death is transformed. Through the power of that Tree, our dying proves a gateway to eternal life, and our misery and despair are transformed into joy. The tree of Marah typified the Tree of the Cross, and the new life-giving waters of Marah proclaim our hope of eternal life.

The Bread from Heaven: Exodus 16

Hunger soon afflicted the people of Israel as they continued their desert journey, and they murmured against their leaders, Moses and Aaron, who had brought them out of Egypt. "You have brought us out into this wilderness," they said, "to kill this whole assembly with hunger" (Ex. 16:3). This was not mere idle grumbling. As the narrative goes on to show in succeeding chapters, such murmuring was the prelude to rebellion, lynching, and a return to Egypt.

Yahweh decided to use their hunger as an opportunity to prove them and teach them to rely on Him. "Behold," He responded, "I will rain bread from heaven for you. And the people shall go out and gather a certain quota every day, that I may test them, whether they will walk in My law or not. And it shall be on the sixth day that they shall prepare what they bring in, and it shall be twice as much as they gather daily" (vv. 4–5). As Yahweh taught them once by miracle and precept at the waters of Marah, so He would teach them by miracle and precept throughout their wilderness wandering. And the first precept He taught them was observance of the Sabbath. He would provide double their daily need on the sixth day, and nothing on the seventh.

The bread from heaven was immediately provided. After the morning dew had gone, the face of the ground was covered by a fine, flakelike substance, fine as hoarfrost, white as coriander seed, sweet as honey. Since it came from heaven as God's provision, later poetry would call it "the food of angels" (Wisdom 16:20). The Israelites gathered the bread with bewilderment, crying, "What is it?" (Heb. *man hu*), a cry which later suggested the name "manna." God would provide it faithfully until they came to the border of the Promised Land. This manna revealed the love and grace and patience of God, for despite Israel's regular outbreaks of rebellion, the provision of heavenly bread never failed. The people's food, life, and strength came from God.

We Christians also experience the faithful provision of heavenly bread that shows God's love and gives us life. Every Sunday, as we assemble for the Eucharist, we partake of Christ, who described Himself as the bread of life (John 6:35), and our Christian life revolves around this weekly eucharistic assembly. It is not surprising that when we read of the manna from heaven that God provided for Israel, we see our own Eucharist, recognizing the manna as a *typos* of our own heavenly Bread. God's provision for Israel in the wilderness of Sinai was a prophecy of His future provision for His Church in the wilderness of the world. God called the children of Israel to gather His bread every day. He calls us to gather the eucharistic bread as often as it is offered. Only by so doing can we have the strength to journey through this dry and barren age to reach our Promised Land.

Moses' Outstretched Arms Bring Victory: Exodus 17:8-16

Thirst and hunger were not the only foes with which Israel had to contend as they marched through the wilderness on the way to Sinai and Canaan. In defiance of all desert codes of decency, the tribe of Amalekites attacked the vulnerable among them at Rephidim (Ex. 17:8). Israel, who as an Egyptian slave force had no military experience, now had to take arms to defend themselves against a skilled aggressor.

For his part, Moses took his stand on the top of a nearby hill with the staff of God in his hand to lift up a prayer to God for victory over the foe. The universal posture for prayer was standing with upraised hands (compare St. Paul's directive in 1 Tim. 2:8 about praying by lifting up holy hands). Accordingly, when Moses lifted up his hands in intercession to God, Israel prevailed against Amalek; but when he ceased from this posture of intercession, letting his hands fall in fatigue by his side, Amalek prevailed. When his attendants Aaron and Hur saw this, they "supported his hands, one on one side, and the other on the other side;

and his hands were steady until the going down of the sun" (Ex. 17:12). The lesson for Israel was plain. If they relied on the power of God, they would have victory over their foes, but if they ceased to rely on Him and relied instead upon their own strength, they would suffer defeat.

Reading this passage from beneath the shadow of the Cross, we discern in it a deeper meaning. We understand its historical message, that victory came only through effective intercession with God. Yet as we read the passage, which portrays a man visible on a hilltop, with his arms outstretched all day into the evening, who by his outstretched arms gave victory and life, we understand something more as well. We remember a Man, visible on a hilltop outside Jerusalem, with His crucified arms outstretched all day into the evening, who by His outstretched arms gave victory over Satan and eternal life.

For us the resemblance of this Mosaic sign of victory to Christ's Cross is not an historical coincidence, but a divine prophecy. Victory over the eternal foes of death, sin, and guilt indeed comes only through God's might, and that might was manifested through the outstretched arms of the crucified Savior, who "always lives to make intercession" for us (Heb. 7:25). The form of the Cross is imprinted on our minds and hearts, and we are sensitized to it. It is inevitable that the striking posture of Moses should foreshadow the Cross of Jesus.

The Rod of Aaron and the Provision of Life: Numbers 16—17

There were other threats to Israel's well-being besides the external threats of the Amalekites. First among these was the rebelliousness of the Israelites themselves. The Books of Exodus, Leviticus, and Numbers are replete with examples of this rebellious spirit, as time and again they rejected and repudiated the gracious provisions of Yahweh. They made a golden calf. Two of Aaron's sons offered strange fire in sacrifice in defiance of God's instructions. The people constantly murmured, grumbling about the miraculous provision of manna, the ascetic difficulties of living in the desert, the challenges of conquering the land of Canaan and overcoming its formidable inhabitants.

The people also grumbled against what they considered the

privileged and exclusive leadership of Moses, and the exclusion from the priesthood of any family but that of Moses' kinsman Aaron. In the words of their rebellious leaders Korah, Dathan, and Abiram to Moses and Aaron, "*You take* too much upon yourselves, for all the congregation *is* holy, every one of them, and the LORD *is* among them. Why then do you exalt yourselves above the assembly of the LORD?" (Num. 16:3). The restriction to Aaron and his family of priesthood with its provisions of food and bestowal of honor was, for them, unwarranted and unconscionable. It was a time of terrible crisis for Moses and Aaron, who were in danger of being stoned. But God sided with them, and the earth swallowed up Korah, Dathan, and Abiram with their families (Num. 16).

But the lesson that God Himself had chosen the family of Aaron for His priests and given the gift of priesthood to them alone still needed to be learned.

> And the LORD spoke to Moses, saying: "Speak to the children of Israel, and get from them a rod from each father's house, all their leaders according to their fathers' houses—twelve rods. Write each man's name on his rod. And you shall write Aaron's name on the rod of Levi. For there shall be one rod for the head of *each* father's house. Then you shall place them in the tabernacle of meeting before the Testimony, where I meet with you. And it shall be *that* the rod of the man whom I choose will blossom; thus I will rid Myself of the complaints of the children of Israel, which they make against you." (Num. 17:1-5)

They did so, and on the day following, "behold, the rod of Aaron, of the house of Levi, had sprouted and put forth buds, had produced blossoms and yielded ripe almonds" (v. 8). By this the lesson was undeniable that Yahweh had chosen the family of Aaron, and them alone, to minister before Him as priests. No other family was chosen, nor would their sacrifices be acceptable. To defy this ruling was to defy Yahweh Himself. The priesthood was, by divine decree, the priesthood of Aaron's family, and life from God came through their sacrifices alone.

Once again, we read this passage with different eyes. That a true and life-giving priesthood and an acceptable sacrifice was revealed through a wooden rod comes as no surprise to us who keep the Cross of Christ always before our eyes. The rod of Aaron was but a dead piece of wood. It was not a living branch, and of itself could not produce living buds and blossoms and fruit. That was why the appearance of buds, blossoms, and fruit was a miracle confirming God's exclusive choice of Aaron. When life came from that dead piece of wood, it showed that Aaron's sacrifice was life-giving.

In the same way, no one seeing Jesus die on the wood thought of that wood as life-giving. The wood of the Cross was not only dead, but deadly. But through the power of God, that wood produced life and beauty and spiritual fruit. For those with eyes to see, it shows that Christ's sacrifice was life-giving. Life-giving wood revealed Aaron as God's true priest to those rebellious men who denied it out of jealousy. In the same way, life-giving wood revealed Jesus as God's true priest. It is His sacrifice of Himself that bears spiritual fruit for all the world. In the rod of Aaron we see a prophecy of the life-giving Cross. We must not rebel against God's provision, as Korah, Dathan, and Abiram did, but look to the Cross alone for salvation.

The Bronze Serpent and Healing the Serpent's Sting: Numbers 21:1–9

Israel's rebellious heart was not easily cured. A few pages after reading of Korah's rebellion against Moses and Aaron, we read of Israel rebelling against that leadership once again. "Why have you brought us up out of Egypt to die in the wilderness? For *there is* no food and no water, and our soul loathes this worthless bread" (Num. 21:5). The "worthless bread" they loathed was the manna God was faithfully sending them from heaven.

In response to such staggering ingratitude, "the LORD sent fiery serpents among the people, and they bit the people; and many of the people of Israel died" (v. 6). These were serpents, peculiar to the east Sinai desert, whose bite produced a painful and lethal inflammation. The people feared they would all die in the desert through this plague, and they repented of their rebellion (the superficiality of their repentance is apparent from the narratives that follow). When they repented, God had mercy on them and undertook to save them from the lethal serpent's sting. "Then the LORD said to Moses, 'Make a fiery *serpent,* and set it on a pole; and it shall be that everyone who is bitten, when he looks at it, shall live.' So Moses made a bronze serpent, and put it on a pole; and so it was, if a serpent had bitten anyone, when he looked at the bronze serpent, he lived" (vv. 8–9).

The serpent is an image of death, and in this story God shows Himself once more to be the Master of life and death, utterly sovereign over the fortunes of men, with power to save Israel and give them health, harvest, and victory when they rely on Him. The use of a serpent's image to absorb the sting of the serpent would resonate with any who knew of sympathetic magic, but this is not so much sympathetic magic as the power of God offered to them in a form they could easily understand. Through the serpent, the serpent's curse was lifted.

The interpretive word of Jesus in the Gospel in John 3:14 reveals the Cross as prophesied in Moses' serpent. The serpent was lifted up on a pole, even as Jesus was lifted up on the Cross. The power of the serpent was its sting, even as the power of sin was the sting of death (see 1 Cor. 15:56). And as the bronze serpent absorbed the serpent's sting, so Christ lifted up on the Cross absorbed death's sting, since He became sin for us (2 Cor. 5:21). The bitten and dying Israelites needed only to look on the bronze serpent to be healed, and sinful and mortal sinners need only look to Christ with faith to be saved. The bronze serpent twisted around a pole and carried to the tents of the dying children of Israel in the desert of Sinai offered a potent prophecy for the Cross of Christ, preached throughout the world to the dying children of men. Our task is to carry the Cross to all the tents of the world, that all may look to Him and be saved.

Balaam and the Prophecies of Power: Numbers 22—24

In Numbers 22—24, we meet Balaam, the son of Beor, a "hired gun" brought in by the local Moabite king Balak and his allies to curse Israel, then encamped in the plains of Moab. Balak saw how soundly Israel had just defeated Sihon, king of the Amorites, and Og, king of Bashan.

Fearful for his own safety, he sent for a famous diviner-seer, a kind of shaman, to inflict a curse on Israel and so make them vulnerable to his military attack. A deputation, richly provided with the fees necessary to hire the diviner, brought him from Pethor, near the Euphrates River.

The story of Balaam's interaction with Balak is recounted with maximum comedic effect. Balaam had his employer build seven altars (the sacred number for oaths and divination) and offer seven bulls and seven rams—a very expensive offering—invoking the divine favor so that the prophet Balaam might receive an oracle to speak an effective curse upon Israel. Balaam does receive the requested prophetic oracle and proclaims it over the people of Israel, but it is a word of blessing, not cursing! Balak is aghast and furious, and decides (in a kind of narrative slapstick) that perhaps the location was the problem. So Balaam has Balak build seven more altars, offer seven more bulls and seven more rams, and wait in the new improved location while he departs to seek for another oracle. It comes, and it is another blessing upon Israel.

Balak is beside himself: "Neither curse them at all, nor bless them at all!" he sputters (Num. 23:25). In other words, "Shut up, if that's all you can do!" Balak's genius solution: Try another location. Another seven altars are built, another seven bulls and another seven rams sacrificed. The response is by now predictable—another blessing.

Balak then explodes in fury, and he claps his hands together in disgust (Num. 24:10). He orders Balaam out of town with threats of violence ("flee to your place," v. 11). Balaam departs, but not before giving one last oracle—this one on the house:

> "The utterance of Balaam the son of Beor,
> And the utterance of the man whose eyes are opened;
> The utterance of him who hears the words of God,
> And has the knowledge of the Most High,
> *Who* sees the vision of the Almighty,
> *Who* falls down, with eyes wide open:
>
> "I see Him, but not now;
> I behold Him, but not near;
> A Star shall come out of Jacob;

A Scepter shall rise out of Israel,
And batter the brow of Moab,
And destroy all the sons of tumult.

"And Edom shall be a possession;
Seir also, his enemies, shall be a possession,
While Israel does valiantly.
Out of Jacob One shall have dominion,
And destroy the remains of the city." (Num. 24:15-19)

There was more to this oracle, all of it bad for Moab, his former employer and would-be benefactor. Then Balaam looked around on Israel's foes and pronounced judgment upon them. Only then "Balaam rose and departed and returned to his place" (Num. 24:25).

The story shows that Israel had nothing to fear from the surrounding nations. Their God was sovereign over all the earth and would protect them from cursing, charms, or magic. If anyone wanted to harm His people, He would stand in their way, nullify the intended harm, and turn curse into blessing. In the oracular words of Balaam, "For *there is* no sorcery against Jacob, / Nor any divination against Israel" (Num. 23:23). Even the pagan diviners are subject to Yahweh's will. He is the *Elyon*, the Most High (Num. 24:16; compare Gen. 14:18), and no god can thwart His will. If He decides to bless Israel, there is nothing any other god or diviner or king can do about it.

The blessings of Balaam focus on Israel's invincibility. From the first oracle in Num. 23:9: "There! A people dwelling alone, / Not reckoning itself among the nations [i.e. as vulnerable as others]." From the second oracle in Num. 23:24: "Look, a people rises like a lioness, / And lifts itself up like a lion; / It shall not lie down until it devours the prey." From the third oracle in Num. 24:8: "[Israel] shall consume the nations, his enemies; / He shall break their bones / And pierce *them* with his arrows." All the oracles proclaim the power of the people of God and their supremacy over the foes that surround them.

These oracles were fulfilled in the rise of the monarchy in Israel, when God gave to the House of David and Solomon power and preeminence among the surrounding nations. Yet for us, the power of the House of David finds its ultimate fulfillment not in any political kingdom, but in Jesus, the messianic Son of David. As the archangel promised the young virgin of Nazareth who was called to be Theotokos, "He will be great, and will be called the Son of the Highest; and the Lord God will give Him the throne of His father David. And He will reign over the house of Jacob forever, and of His kingdom there will be no end" (Luke 1:32–33).

This Kingdom is the ultimate fulfillment of the glory foreseen by Balaam long ago in the plains of Moab. Jesus is the king whom he "beheld," though He was then "not near." He is the final "Star" that "shall come out of Jacob," the "Scepter" that "shall rise out of Israel." It is not surprising that a star appeared in heaven at the birth of Jesus, for Jesus Himself was the Star that came forth from Jacob. Whatever his personal failings, Balaam accurately foresaw the glory of the people of Israel that found its eternal culmination in the Kingdom of Christ.

The Sacrifices Offered Within the Holy Tents: Exodus and Leviticus

The beating heart of the Mosaic covenant was the Ark of God and the altars that stood before it. The tent curtains Israel erected at the command of God through Moses concealed the place where God met with His people and blessed them. On the mountaintop of Sinai, Moses received detailed instructions for the divine cultus—how to build the Ark of God and enclose it within the tents of the inmost Holy of Holies; how to build the seven-branched lampstand, the table for the showbread, and the golden altar for burning incense; and how to enclose them within the Holy Place that surrounded the Holy of Holies. He was instructed how to build a bronze altar for offering the sacrifices and a bronze laver or bath for washing the priests and their sacrifices. He was told how to make the frames and the curtains that hung on them, which enclosed the entire sanctuary, including the bronze altar and the laver that stood before the Holy Place, under the open sky. He was told how to make the vestments for the high priest and his assistants, the other priests. He was told how to ordain them so they could offer sacrifice (literally, how to "fill their hand"). He was told how to make the incense and the anointing oil. He was given detailed instructions regarding how and when to offer sacrifices. All that was needed for a functioning priesthood and the offering of sacrifice throughout the year, Moses was given by God on Mount Sinai.

The other laws were, in a sense, subordinate to these instructions. We who are heirs of the Enlightenment can miss this. We tend easily to reduce religion to ethical injunctions and to regard the laws regulating behavior as the real point of the Law, dismissing the instructions for a functioning priesthood as mere indulgence to the all-too-limited understanding of primitive men. Israelites, like all primitive men of that time (this view asserts), felt they needed an altar and a priesthood, and so God provided these for them as a concession to their childish ways. But we who are mature see that sacrifice has nothing to do with real religion. Real religion consists of ethical instructions about justice and social concerns.

A careful reading of the Law suggests otherwise. The heart of the Law—its central purpose—was to have God dwelling in the midst of His people, like the fire that burned within the unconsumed bush. He dwelt among them so they could approach Him and receive His blessing, and this approach was always through sacrifice. The other laws regulating behavior were given so they might safely and fruitfully make that approach. Ethics were not irrelevant to sacrificial worship (as pagans of Moses' day and since have thought). God gave Israel the "ethical" laws governing their behavior, not because keeping those laws was an end in itself, but so that their behavior might not disqualify them from approaching Him.

We find this image of the divine indwelling throughout the Law. God led Israel by the pillar of cloud by day and the pillar of fire by night. When the Ark and all the cultus of priesthood were ready, God came to dwell among them through His Presence with the Ark. "So Moses finished the work. Then the cloud covered the tabernacle of meeting, and the glory of the LORD filled the tabernacle" (Ex. 40:33–34). Henceforth the Ark, a traveling shrine, would be the locus of God's Presence with them. They encamped around it during their wilderness wandering, like an army encamping around its king

(Numbers 2 gives the actual tribal arrangements for such a camp).

This sense of encamping around the Ark in their midst continued once Israel's wilderness wandering was over and they were living in the Promised Land. God said He would choose a place "out of all your tribes, to put His name for His dwelling place; and there you shall go" (Deut. 12:5). The place might be at Shiloh or elsewhere, but wherever the place was, Israel would make that location the center of their national existence. Three times a year the people must bring their sacrifices there and keep a feast (these were the feasts of Passover, Weeks, and Booths). The technical name for this type of life is an "amphictony"—a loose confederation of tribes uniting to defend a common religious center, that center being the shrine containing the Ark. Israel was a united people only because they had Yahweh dwelling in their midst in those sacred tents. All of the provisions of the Law, including the ones we regard as distinctly "ethical" as opposed to "cultic," had as their goal holy men standing within those tents and offering sacrifice to God.

We moderns have never offered sacrifice as the ancients did. For them, religion *was* sacrifice—taking a living, breathing animal, cutting its throat, catching the blood in bowls and basins and throwing it against an altar, skinning and slaughtering the animal and offering it up as a burnt offering (or possibly eating some of the roast meat themselves). It was through this act of sacrifice that a worshipper communed with his deity and sought divine blessing. If this seems odd or unnatural to us, it only shows how far we have traveled from the understanding of the ancients.

This understanding of worship, common to both Jews and pagans, is presupposed by the writers of the New Testament. For the apostolic leaders as for the Israelites of old, worship did not consist simply of praise or prayer. Praise and prayer found their context in sacrifice, and it was sacrifice that gave the praise and prayer a saving potency. The idea of religion without sacrifice was to them simply a contradiction in terms. That is why Israel was in such anguish when they lost the Temple and the possibility of sacrifice in the Babylonian Exile, and why they were so urgent in their desire to have it restored (compare Daniel's prayer in Daniel 9). The rabbis after the catastrophic loss of the Temple in AD 70 tried to construct a religion without the necessity of sacrifice, but such rabbinic Judaism bore faint resemblance to the Mosaic religion of the Old Testament. Communion with God, in the Old Testament, was only possible through sacrifice.

Having said this, we believe that these animal sacrifices were insufficient to resolve the human condition and heal the hearts of men. Having experienced Christ's power to strengthen the will, to cleanse and transfigure the human person inside and out, we look upon the sacrifices of the Law as fundamentally deficient and inadequate. Such sacrifices might remove a merely ceremonial impurity, but they were powerless to remove the deeper impurity of the heart. As the Epistle to the Hebrews says, those sacrifices "cannot make him who performed the service perfect in regard to the conscience—*concerned* only with foods and drinks, various washings, and fleshly ordinances." Certainly "the blood of bulls and goats and the ashes of a heifer, sprinkling the unclean, sanctifies for the purifying of the flesh." But they "can never... make those who approach perfect. For then would they not have ceased to be offered?... For *it is* not possible that the blood of bulls and goats could take away sins" (Heb. 9:9–10, 13; 10:1–4).

The writer to the Hebrews calls attention to the universal experience of all who have ever offered sacrifice—that such sacrifices leave the human heart untouched and unhealed. The Law's multitude of sacrifices can *express the desire* for inner healing and cleansing, but cannot *bestow* it. Animal sacrifices can cleanse the flesh, removing merely external uncleanness that defiles the outward body. But human beings crave something more; we long for a peace and a purity beyond what animal sacrifice can offer. We believers experience that longed-for peace and cleansing through Christ and His Sacrifice on the Cross, and so we regard all the Old Testament sacrifices as prophecies of that Sacrifice. Jesus is the true Sacrifice, foreshadowed by the many offerings of the Law. All the Mosaic provisions of Ark, altars, tents, priesthood, and sacrifice find their fulfillment in Him.

An Angels'-Eye View of Worship Within the Tents

The establishment through Moses of the whole cultus of Ark, sacred Tents, priesthood, and sacrifice was a great gift to Israel. Just as children receive gifts of love from their father with joy, so Israel received this gift with exultation and delight. Some of this delight we see reflected in the description of the high priest Simon, son of Onias, found in Sirach 50:11–17:

> When he took up a robe of honor
> And was clothed with the perfection of boasting
> In his ascent to the holy altar,
> He glorified the court of the sanctuary.
> When he received the portion from the hands of the priests
> While standing by the hearth of the altar,
> A crown of brethren surrounding him,
> He was like a sapling of cedar in Lebanon;
> And they encircled him like the trunks of palm trees,
> All the sons of Aaron in their glory,
> And the offering to the Lord in their hands
> Before all the assembly of Israel.
> Finishing the services at the altars
> And arranging the offering to the Most High, the Almighty,
> He stretched out his hand to the cup
> And poured a libation of the blood of the grapes.
> He poured it out on the foundation of the altar,
> A fragrant scent to the King of all, the Most High.
> Then the sons of Aaron cried out,
> Sounding out the trumpets of hammered work,
> A great noise to be heard
> As a remembrance before the Most High.
> Then all the people hastened in common
> And fell with their faces on the ground
> To worship their Lord, the Almighty God, the Most High.

As the Psalmist said centuries before:

> How lovely *is* Your tabernacle,
> O LORD of hosts!
> My soul longs, yes, even faints

For the courts of the LORD;
My heart and my flesh cry out for the living God. (Ps. 84:1-2)

No one can begin to understand the provisions for the altar and its sacrifices who does not keep in mind this ancient delight and joy.

And yet, notwithstanding Israel's delight in its Temple service, we still see a discontinuity between the glory of this earthly worship and the full glory of God. All the ancients knew this, of course. They knew that their deity or deities were not confined within their temples as shoes in a shoebox. When they pondered the question (many of course didn't), they knew that deity was something greater, and that their earthly temples were mere reflections of the deity's true dwelling in heaven.

The concept of the earthly reflecting the heavenly did not begin with Plato and his "forms" and "ideas." All the ancients knew the earthly temples for their gods were models and approximations of the heavenly realities. This included the Jews. The writer of the Epistle to the Hebrews refers to this common understanding when he writes that Moses was warned by God to "make all things [for the Tabernacle] according to the pattern [Greek *typos*, "type"] shown you on the mountain" (Heb. 8:5). That is, Jews believed that on Mount Sinai Moses received a vision of the transcendent glory of God in His heavenly dwelling place, and that the Tabernacle he erected was to reflect this glory. The heavenly glory formed the pattern, the *typos*, which the earthly Tabernacle was to reflect.

Thus even according to the Law, the heavenly glory of God was greater than the earthly glory of the Tabernacle and its cultus. We can begin to see how much greater when we stop and look at that cultus from the viewpoint of the angels—or, if not the angels, at least the religious sociologists. From the historical sociological view, it is apparent that the tents prescribed by Moses had their origin in the tent dwellings of the Bedouin (such as Abraham and the patriarchs).

Those tent dwellings contained an inner space for the women's quarters and an outer part of the tent for the men to greet their visitors. Surrounding this was a courtyard, where the Bedouin's animals might be. The basic pattern conforms to the tripartite structure of the Mosaic tents, with the inner Holy of Holies answering to the women's quarters, the outer Holy Place answering to the men's quarters where visitors were received, and the outer courtyard where the altar stood answering to the Bedouin's courtyard. The Mosaic shrine thus was an adaptation of the normal tents used for daily living. The writer of the Epistle to the Hebrews alludes to this prosaic aspect of the shrine when he points out that it contained such everyday items as were found in a normal home—a lampstand, a table, and bread (Heb. 9:2). The courts of the Lord, for all their glory, had a very earthy and humble character.

The angels, from their heavenly viewpoint, behold God in His heavenly Temple. Such is the heavenly glory that the fiery seraphim cover their faces before God, crying out in awe, "Holy, holy, holy *is* the LORD of hosts; / The whole earth *is* full of His glory!" (Is. 6:3). Not even these angels are clean in His sight, in that even they cannot serve Him as He deserves (Job 15:15). He who created the vast expanse of interstellar space, who holds the entire universe in His hand as a man could hold a walnut—this mighty, transcendent God chose to make His covenant dwelling in the tents of primitive nomads.

The people of Israel were a humble people, even as the Law declares (Deut. 7:7)—culturally primitive, unskilled in worldly wisdom, industry, or craft. In their desert wandering, they constructed at the divine command a box of wood, about four feet by two feet by two feet, and adorned it with hammered gold plate. A few other items were similarly constructed. The priests officiating at the portable altar were dressed in whatever finery their primitive industry and skill could provide. And this, doubtless to the astonishment of the angels, was where God chose to dwell in all the earth. King David, himself culturally primitive by later standards, recognized with embarrassment the humility of the divine cult and thought to build a more fitting dwelling for it (2 Sam. 7:2). The Temple his son Solomon built, though more splendid than the simple Mosaic shrine, still was sadly incommensurate with the divine glory—as Solomon himself confessed at the consecration of the Temple (1 Kin. 8:27). In the tents erected by Moses, the divine humility shines forth.

For us who have seen the glory of God shining in the face of Jesus, the simplicity of the Mosaic tents is a prophecy of the humility of Christ. Christ indeed was humble, a carpenter from Nazareth, a city of which it was proverbially said, "Can anything good come from Nazareth?" He had no worldly connections with important people, no vast resources, not even a place to lay His head. His followers were women, tax-collectors, sinners, people of the land. Some in His day thought it inconceivable that such a humble person could be the Messiah. But we know that the divine humility which was content to attach its transcendent and glorious Name to humble nomadic tents would not scruple to become incarnate in a humble carpenter. The divine glory always veils itself in this age—whether behind the literal veils of a rustic desert shrine or in the human flesh of a Jewish peasant. The humble rusticity of the Mosaic shrine points ahead to the voluntary humility of the coming Messiah.

The Abiding Significance of the Law

The Law was God's supreme gift to the Jewish people, the prism through which they could discern His will and learn the desires of His heart. It was never meant as the means through which they could win merit or earn His love. It was not necessary for them to earn His love, for that love was already freely given when He brought them out of Egypt to His holy mountain. The deliverance from Egyptian bondage was a gift of grace, and the Law was given within the context of that grace.

God wanted a relationship of love with His people. He wanted them to love Him in response to His love for them. The Law revealed how they were to give that love—by worshiping no other gods but Him, by treating their neighbors justly, by showing kindness to the stranger, the widow, and the orphan. Loving Him meant living chaste lives of faithfulness to spouses. It meant showing gratitude to parents and respect for the old. Loving Him meant treating even animals kindly (see Deut. 22:6-7; 25:4); it meant not destroying the environment unnecessarily (see Deut. 20:19-20). It meant caring for slaves, even to the point of freeing them after six years' service, and forgiving all debts in the year of jubilee. The Law revealed God's love of justice, chastity, kindness, and liberty. God loved these things and wanted His people to love them too.

But though the Law could reveal this shining ideal, it could not impart it. As St. Paul would later point out, if a man remained in bondage to sin, an addict to covetousness for example, merely saying, "Do not covet!" could not free him from a covetous spirit (Rom. 7:7f). The Law remained external, carved on stones, stored in the Ark. God could write the Law on the tablets for Moses; the history of Israel's ongoing apostasy proved it was not thereby written on the hearts of His people. That task was not given to Moses; it was the work of the Holy Spirit after the glorification of Christ. But now that the Spirit of Christ does write the Law into the hearts of His Christian people, the Law abides in the Church as an invaluable gift, holding forth the ideals of justice, chastity, kindness, and liberty which the power of the Spirit helps us fulfill.

CHAPTER 3

THE HISTORICAL BOOKS:
LIVING IN THE LAND

An Overview of the Historical Books

THE HISTORICAL BOOKS OF THE OLD TESTAMENT record the adventures of Israel and their interactions with the Lord as they lived in the Promised Land as God's covenant people. This long and sweeping saga begins in the Book of Joshua as Israel crosses the border of Canaan and begins the long struggle to conquer the land as God commanded. After the death of Joshua, it became an uneven struggle as Israel alternated between faithfulness and apostasy, and therefore between victory and defeat, experiencing the ebb and flow of advance and retreat. This ebb and flow is recorded in the Book of Judges, as Israel retreated in defeat and disgrace, then repented, and then experienced victory as God raised up a series of judges, or freedom fighters. It was a time of chaos, when every man did what was right in his own eyes (Judg. 21:25).

This constant threat of death and defeat at the hands of Canaanite neighbors induced Israel to ask for a dynastic king with a standing army. Under the Judges, leaders were non-dynastic and did not leave a successor behind them when they died. The armies of Israel were more like militia, peasant farmers who took to arms to meet an urgent threat. Under pressure from better-armed and technologically superior neighbors, Israel wanted the abiding security that came from having a king like all the other nations (1 Sam. 8:4–5). God acquiesced, and through Samuel gave them a dynastic king.

Monarchy proved to be a mixed blessing. Some kings were good and kept God's Law, but some were not, straying into idolatry and thereby bringing disaster on the nation. God sent prophets during these days of idolatry, warning king and commoner alike to serve Yahweh alone, but their voices were too seldom heeded. Eventually the tribes were swept away by the surrounding pagan nations, as God had warned through His Law they would be if they continued to rebel against Him. First the northern kingdom of Israel was swept away by the Assyrians, and then the southern kingdom of Judah faced national annihilation at the hands of the Babylonians. For a long lifetime (a proverbial seventy years), they languished in exile. And then, like the prodigal son, they came to themselves and repented.

God had not only promised in His Law that if they sinned He would banish them from His presence (i.e. from the Promised Land), He also promised that He would regather them to the land if they turned back to Him. Accordingly, after the exile the nation was reborn, like dry bones coming together and rising from the dead (see Ezekiel 37). Through the work of Ezra and Nehemiah, a small foothold was reestablished in the land of Judah, and Israel was once more a people in the land. There, surrounded by more powerful and intimidating neighbors, they hoped for better times.

These better times had a name: the Messiah. One of their best kings was David, himself a general under Saul, the first king. Unlike Saul, David had a heart for God and loved Him, despite his occasional lapses. When David wanted to build God a House (a temple) worthy of His greatness, God responded that, on the contrary, *He* would build *David* a house—not a physical temple, but an enduring dynasty. Other kings might come and go, but David's dynasty would endure forever (2 Sam. 7). When the southern kingdom fell, David's descendants fell with it, and there was no king in Judah any more. But God's promise remained, and all Israel looked to God to keep His word and restore one of David's descendants to the promised former greatness. So it was that the fledgling nation taking shape around Jerusalem looked to the future. The experience of living in the land became fused with prophetic hope.

Joshua and the Conquest of Canaan: Joshua 1—4

The people that left Egypt were not so much a single nation as a collection of disparate tribes, each one proud of its independence and keen to war against other tribes—as the later history of those wars related in Judges 20—21 testifies. Each man thought of himself primarily as a member of his tribe, and only secondarily as a part of the larger covenant people of Israel. These tribes did not regard themselves as their brother's keeper. When Deborah sang her song praising intertribal cooperation in Judges 3, she reserved some verses to blame those tribes that stood aloof from the military conflict that engaged others.

This sense of tribal independence was only slowly worn down and might flare up like a fever at any moment. (We see such a flare-up in 1 Kings 12, when the northern tribes repudiated the tribe of Judah and its king, Rehoboam, grandson of King David, for favoring his own tribe at their expense.) The people of Israel had little sense of nationhood during their long, grinding bondage in Egypt. That sense of being a single people was only given to them by God at Mount Sinai, when the covenant was made between God and the people as a whole (and even then, Moses' own tribe of Levi was perceived by the other tribes as being treated with undeserved favoritism). It would take many wars and the combined effort of kings and prophets to forge any sense of unity among the tribes.

The Book of Joshua was not just an historical record, but a clarion call to this unity. Over and over again, we read there about "the people of Israel," and tribal divisions are mentioned only to underscore this basic unity of the people. Thus, in the very first chapter, the tribes that were settled beyond the Jordan under Moses pass on ahead of the other tribes so that they all invade Canaan together as one army. As Joshua commanded these Trans-Jordanian tribes, "But you shall pass before your brethren armed, all your mighty men of valor, and help them, until the LORD has given your brethren rest, as He *gave* you, and they also have taken possession of the land which the LORD your God is giving them" (Josh. 1:14–15). The Trans-Jordanian tribes could not separate themselves from the other tribes simply because they already possessed their tribal allotments of the land. In the time of the conquest under Joshua, it had to be "all for one and one for all."

We see the same concern for pan-tribal unity as they crossed the Jordan: When God stopped the flowing water of the river, allowing them to cross over the border of Canaan dry shod, twelve stones were taken from the river bottom so that a cairn could be erected on the river bank in memorial of this miracle (Joshua 3—4). The twelve stones made a single memorial, even as all the tribes together experienced God's power and functioned as a single nation.

The Book of Joshua concludes in chapter 22 by holding forth the same shining beacon of intertribal unity. The western tribes found in the midst of the tribes east of the Jordan what they thought was a rival altar. The erection of such an altar would be an act of tribal defiance and apostasy, for Yahweh had declared that all the twelve tribes in covenant with Him were to resort to the central shrine set up under Moses. This rival altar thus represented schism and sacrifice to another god. When challenged at spear point, the tribes east of the Jordan responded that they had built the altar in their midst not as a functioning altar for sacrifice, but simply as a replica of the one true altar before the Ark, as an enduring witness that the Trans-Jordanian tribes were one with the others, even though the Jordan River seemed to form a border separating them (vv. 21–29). Their intention was not schism, but on the contrary, abiding unity. This unity would form the foundation for future military victory and survival.

We Christians reading the Book of Joshua consider ourselves as the heirs of its victories, since the Church is "the commonwealth of Israel" and "the Israel of God" (Eph. 2:12; Gal. 6:16). And what strikes us first and forcibly in their reading is the name of its protagonist—in Hebrew Yehoshua (יהושע), and in Greek ἰήσους—Anglicized as "Jesus." The fact that the people of God were led to victory in the Promised Land by Jesus inevitably suggests a fruitful typology.

The promised Land of Canaan typified the promise of eternal life, "the land of the living" (Ps. 27:13). Even as Israelites were brought by the death of the paschal lamb and through Red Sea baptism into Canaan, even so we Christians are brought by the death of the paschal Lamb of God and through sacramental baptism into the Kingdom. The Epistle to the Hebrews makes this typology explicit in its fourth chapter, where it declares that the "rest" referred to in Psalm 95:11 points ultimately not to the Israelites' rest in Canaan, but to their rest in the Kingdom of God, the true Sabbath. Regarding the final rest from the labors of this age, it says, "There remains therefore a rest for the people of God. For he who has entered His rest has himself also ceased from his works as God *did* from His. Let us therefore be diligent to enter that rest, lest anyone fall according to the same example of disobedience" (Heb. 4:9–11). Christians journeying through the spiritual desert of this age are heading for the Promised Land no less than the Israelites who journeyed through the Sinai. And as Jesus the son of Nun led them to that Promised Land, so Jesus the Son of Man leads us to ours. Joshua is a potent *typos* of the Savior Jesus.

This prophetic identity of Joshua with Jesus suggests a further typological truth, that of the ineffectiveness of Moses and Judaism. In the Law and the Historical Books, Moses was not allowed to enter the Promised Land because of his sin. As Moses himself said to Israel, "The LORD was also angry with me for your sakes, saying, 'Even you shall not go in there. Joshua the son of Nun, who stands before you, he shall go in there. Encourage him, for he shall cause Israel to inherit it'" (Deut. 1:37–38).

Moses was referring to his disobedience to God's word by the waters of Meribah, recorded in Numbers 20, when God said, "Because you did not believe Me, to hallow Me in the eyes of the children of Israel, therefore you shall not bring this assembly into the land which I have given them" (v. 12). Moses was God's man, and the Law he brought Israel was a divine gift, but his lack of faith and his sin disqualified him from entering Canaan. It was his successor, Jesus the son of Nun, who brought Israel into Canaan.

In the same way, the Law of Moses and the Judaism based on it cannot bring men into the Kingdom. Only acceptance of what came after the Law, the Gospel of Jesus, can bring men into the Kingdom of God. The relationship between Moses and Joshua typifies that of the Law and the Gospel.

The typology that sees in the land of Canaan an image of the Kingdom also gives deeper meaning to the Jordan River, which forms the geographical boundary of Canaan (as the Trans-Jordanian tribes knew very well; compare Joshua 22). To enter Canaan, Israel had to cross the Jordan River; to enter the Kingdom, we need to cross the boundary of death. Meditating on this, we can take comfort in the story of Joshua 3—4, which relates how God brought Israel miraculously across the Jordan so that they crossed dry shod. In the same way, God will bring us safely across this final barrier into His Presence in the heavenly Kingdom. This comforting typology has found its way into one of the old African-American spirituals, "Michael, row your boat ashore":

> River Jordan is muddy and cold, Hallelujah!
> Chills the body, but not the soul, Hallelujah!

This spiritual, which asks the archangel Michael for safe conduct across the river of death, has deep roots in the classic Christian typology of Joshua and Jesus. For us, the story of Jesus the son of Nun speaks of our own spiritual warfare and entry into the promised Kingdom. We need not fear the crossing of the chilly Jordan, the final border between us and our destination. God saw Israel safely to Canaan, and His power will see us safely home as well.

David and Goliath: 1 Samuel 17

David appears in the historical books as the successor to King Saul. God chose David as a man after His own heart to take Saul's place after the latter's apostasy from God and death on Mount Gilboa while fighting the Philistines. David shines in the historical chronicles as a beloved and ideal king—one who rose to kingship on his popularity with the common people, and who even in old age continued to inspire love and loyalty in those near to him. He founded an enduring dynasty that continued to reign in the southern kingdom of Judah even after the northern tribes that defected from the leadership of his house were swept away into exile by the Assyrians.

Despite the sins of David's descendants on the throne, God said He would continue to bless the kingdom for David's sake, "that My servant

David may always have a lamp before Me in Jerusalem" (1 Kings 11:36). Scripture relates three high points in David's life. The first is the story of his youthful victory when he slew the giant Goliath in a dramatic encounter and turned the tide in Israel's conflict with the Philistines. The famous story is related in 1 Samuel 17.

The tale is one of the most beloved in Scripture and has become a proverbial image in popular culture for a fight between two wildly unequal contestants. For Israel, the victory of the young and inexperienced shepherd boy over the older and battle-hardened warrior had its own national resonance. Israel also felt itself young and inexperienced, surrounded on all sides by large and militarily superior enemies who despised them as Goliath despised David. Against such foes, their only hope was the help of God. Their foes might come to the battlefield with sword, spear, and javelin, with all the experience and technology found in empires and superpowers. Israel came to the battle "in the name of the LORD of hosts, the God of the armies of Israel" (1 Sam. 17:45). Yet despite the superiority of their foes, Israel was taught by young David's example that they could expect victory from God.

As we read this story, we are confronted by other enemies. The invincible foe we face is not Goliath, nor any champion of an enemy nation, for we Christians are not national, with national boundaries and a national army, but international, drawn "of all nations, tribes, peoples, and tongues" (Rev. 7:9). The terrifying foe we face is the devil, who has the power of death (Heb. 2:14). When we read of David, we see our own Lord, who was descended from David, whose messianic title is "Son of David" and who is called "David" in the writings of the prophets (compare Ezek. 34:23). Jesus came to battle on behalf of His people, who trembled in fear of the gigantic Enemy from a distance, not daring to go out to meet the foe. And like David, who went to the fight armed only with a shepherd's sling and five smooth stones newly chosen from the brook, Jesus ran quickly to the battle line and killed the giant foe with a single slung stone.

As David slew Goliath with a single stone, so Christ slew the devil with His single death. And what of those precious five stones the story of David mentions (v. 40)? What else could they be but the five precious wounds of Christ in His hands and His side, with which He "trampled down death by death, upon those in the tombs bestowing life"? With the death of Goliath, all Philistine opposition melted away as the Philistines fled in fear (v. 51). With the death of the Savior Christ, the Son of David, all demonic opposition flees away as well, as Christ gives us the victory over Satan and death.

Christians see in the story of David and Goliath the victory Jesus has won for them at the Cross. The certainty of physical death may sound terrifying in our ears, as did the boasts of Goliath in the ears of Saul's army, for the giant threatened destruction to all who came near. But we need fear nothing. Christ has "trampled down death, and overthrown the devil, and given life to His world." We can have peace even in the face of death, trusting in our mighty Champion.

David and the Ark: 2 Samuel 6

The second high point in David's life was his transfer of the sacred Ark to his newly founded citadel in Zion,[3] which became "the city of David." Formerly the Ark had been left in the house of Abinadab at Kiriath-jearim after its recovery from the Philistines. The Ark formed the hub around which all Israel gathered and to which they would come to offer sacrifice. It was therefore the center of the nation's religious life.

In a stroke of political genius, David decided to unite the religious and civil life of the nation by bringing the Ark into his capital and headquarters, so that all Israel would come to his own city to offer sacrifice. David's city thereby became the hub around which the people of Israel would revolve. As the Psalmist would later sing:

> Jerusalem is built
> As a city that is compact together,
> Where the tribes go up,
> The tribes of the LORD,
> To the Testimony of Israel,

---

[3] "Zion" means "height," referring to its hilltop location.

> To give thanks to the name of the Lord.
> For thrones are set there for judgment,
> The thrones of the house of David. (Ps. 122:3–5)

Israel was to find its national unity around him.

The story is told in 2 Samuel 6. "So David went and brought up the ark of God from the house of Obed-Edom to the City of David with gladness.... Then David danced before the Lord with all *his* might; and David *was* wearing a linen ephod" (vv. 12–14). Though the people shared David's exuberance and joy in having God dwelling in his city, his wife Michal, the daughter of his dead rival King Saul, did not. She "looked through a window and saw King David leaping and whirling before the Lord; and she despised him in her heart" (v. 16).

When he returned home, Michal rebuked her royal husband, saying, "How glorious was the king of Israel today, uncovering himself today in the eyes of the maids of his servants, as one of the base fellows shamelessly uncovers himself!" (v. 20). It was not the way a wife of that time should address her husband, much less her king. Doubtless she still smarted from the death of her father Saul and resented David's displacement of him. In her eyes, Saul acted like a true king, keeping his dignity intact, and did not let himself get carried away before the common people. David should be more like Saul.

David did not think so and turned on her with a just rebuke: "*It was* before the Lord, who chose me instead of your father and all his house, to appoint me ruler over the people of the Lord, over Israel. Therefore I will play *music* before the Lord. And I will be even more undignified than this, and will be humble in my own sight. But as for the maidservants of whom you have spoken, by them I will be held in honor." David did not think his humility and self-forgetfulness was improper for a king. He was content to be humble if only he could rejoice in the Lord. The writer of the narrative records God's view of their quarrel: "Therefore Michal the daughter of Saul had no children to the day of her death" (vv. 21–23). She was barren ever after, as a judgment from God.

As said above, we Christians find in David a type of Christ, and the self-forgetful humility of David, contrasting with the haughty pride of the House of Saul, speaks of the humility of Christ. Christ came to His own in humility, clad not in a linen ephod, but in human flesh, and His own despised Him and did not receive Him (John 1:11).

Like Saul's proud daughter Michal, Israel could not accept a humble Messiah, one without military power or aspirations, one who did not wrangle or cry aloud with a battle cry, or make His voice heard in the streets of the world (Is. 42:2; Matt. 12:19). Israel despised Him for His humility, for welcoming tax-collectors and sinners, for a poverty that had nowhere to lay its head (Matt. 8:20; 9:11). It wanted a Messiah like King Saul, conscious of his own dignity in the eyes of the world.

Yet Christ refused the way of power and pride, preferring to be held in honor by the humble, the sinners, the maidservants of Israel who were disdained by the proud. Indeed, He determined "to be even more undignified than this"—accepting not only human flesh at the Incarnation, but also death in disgrace upon a cross. By rejecting the humble Christ, Israel, like Saul's daughter, doomed itself to a future of spiritual barrenness. In David's dance of self-forgetful joy before the Ark and in his exchange with Michal, we see the Incarnation of Christ and the doomed sterility of Judaism.

David and the Undying Promise: 2 Samuel 7

The third high point of David's life was his desire to build a House for his Lord. When his kingdom was secure and the Ark of God had been safely installed in his capital, he felt keenly how humble and rustic were the dwellings of the God of the whole earth. He therefore said to Nathan, his court prophet and advisor, "See now, I dwell in a house of cedar, but the ark of God dwells inside tent curtains" (2 Sam. 7:2). His intention was to build God a house more in keeping with His dignity and glory. Nathan (a bit prematurely, as it turned out) blessed David to proceed with his desire.

But God was no one's debtor. It could not be that anyone should think David somehow did a favor for God. On the contrary, God was the One who favored David, taking him from the pasture, from following the sheep, to be prince over His people, cutting off his enemies,

The Historical Books

and making for him a great name (vv. 8-9). David would not build a house for God; God would build one for him. That is, God promised to bless David's dynasty after him, never taking away the kingship from his descendants, no matter what their sins. He might have judged Saul in that way, removing him and his descendants from the throne, but He would not deal so with David. Judgments would come if David's descendants sinned. But God would keep His word to establish the throne of David's kingdom forever (vv. 11-13). This promise became the foundation of Israel's messianic hope.

That hope was severely challenged by the Babylonian Exile, and that traumatic challenge is reflected in Psalms 88 and 89 (which form a matched set). Psalm 88 is a lament, a cry of one man's dereliction and feeling of being abandoned by God. His soul is full of troubles; he draws near to the pit of death. He is as good as dead, and God's help is long overdue.

> My eye wastes away because of affliction.
> LORD, I have called daily upon You;
> I have stretched out my hands to You.
> Will You work wonders for the dead?
> Shall the dead arise *and* praise You? (Ps. 88:9-10)

God will not come to save him. He will die waiting for His help. The psalm ends on a hopeless note (the only one to do so in the entire Psalter): "Loved one and friend You have put far from me, / *And* my acquaintances into darkness" (Ps. 88:18). It is a dark psalm, full of despair. No wonder the Church chose this psalm to express the despair felt at the death of Christ, using verse 6 as a prokeimenon for Holy Friday Vespers: "You have laid me in the depths of the pit, in regions dark and deep."

Psalm 88 is paired with another psalm by a fellow Ezrahite, because it is ultimately not just about the despair of a dying man but also about the despair of a dead nation, one abandoned by God and living in exile. Psalm 89 makes this explicit. The first part rehearses God's unfailing promise to David and his descendants that the kingdom over which he reigns will never fail.

For I have said, "Mercy shall be built up forever;
Your faithfulness You shall establish in the very heavens."
"I have made a covenant with My chosen,
I have sworn to My servant David:
'Your seed I will establish forever,
And build up your throne to all generations.'" (Ps. 89:2–4)

The psalmist recounts the glory of David in great detail, since it was the gift of God.

The enemy shall not outwit him,
Nor the son of wickedness afflict him.
I will beat down his foes before his face . . .
Also I will set his hand over the sea,
And his right hand over the rivers. . . .
Also I will make him *My* firstborn,
The highest of the kings of the earth.
. . .
His seed shall endure forever,
And his throne as the sun before Me;
It shall be established forever like the moon,
Even *like* the faithful witness in the sky. (Ps. 89:22–27, 36–37)

Then, in the second part, comes the cry of confusion and despair. The descendant of David, King Zedekiah, had indeed been outwitted by the enemy, and the wicked did humble him. The king of Babylon captured him, slew his sons before him before gouging out his eyes, and took him in chains to Babylon. Far from him being "the highest of the kings of the earth," God had "turned back the edge of his sword, . . . made his glory cease, / And cast his throne down to the ground" (Ps. 89:43–44). It seemed as if God had lied, and His promises to David for an eternal throne had proved utterly false.

Yet after Israel returned from exile, they still treasured these words and hoped that God would yet restore a descendant of David to the throne and make him as glorious as Psalm 89 promised. The king anointed by God would yet come forth and bring an eternal kingdom with its capital in Jerusalem. Postexilic Israel believed in this kingdom and impatiently awaited it.

We see that God's promises for an eternal kingdom were never meant to have a political, military, or worldly fulfillment. Kingdoms rise and fall; they come and go. Even the Roman Empire of Byzantium, which endured over a thousand years, finally fell in 1453. The Kingdom of God, however, would arise and never fall, for it is not of this world. Its capital is not Jerusalem in Palestine, but the heavenly Jerusalem; its Messiah King sits not on an earthly throne, protected by armies, but at the right hand of God, protected by God's invincible might.

Almost a thousand years before Jesus was born, God entered into a covenant with a desert guerrilla-become-king called David. In response to David's devotion, God decided to make an undying covenant with him, one that would be the vehicle for His eternal Kingdom. Here we behold the depths of God's condescension and wisdom. The covenant was rooted in history, and seemed to promise only an enduring earthly dynasty. No doubt David, hearing God's promise, thought only that his line was to be more secure than that of his predecessor Saul. He had no inkling of the full and final fulfillment of the covenant and of how history would coalesce with eternity.

The national existence of Israel served an historical purpose, but came to an end a generation after the rejection and crucifixion of Christ. But the promise made long ago to David was destined to outlast that nation and to become the undying instrument for the salvation of the world.

Elijah and Elisha and the Miracles of the Remnant: 1 and 2 Kings

After David, Solomon sat on his throne, amassing immense riches and leaving a legacy of splendor. "All King Solomon's drinking vessels *were* gold, and all the vessels of the House of the Forest of Lebanon *were* pure gold. Not *one was* silver, for this was accounted as nothing in the days of Solomon" (1 Kin. 10:21). Such splendor came at a cost, of course, which was crushing taxation (a phenomenon not unknown today).

In the days of Solomon's successor Rehoboam, the people of Israel protested the burden of taxation and forced labor and asked King Rehoboam to lighten it. He hearkened to the voice of his contemporaries rather than his elders. These young advisors counseled a show of strength, saying that he should refuse the people's demands. Rehoboam therefore defied the tribal delegation, telling them he would in fact increase their burden rather than lighten it. He would show them!

In exasperation, the northern tribes repudiated the monarchy of the House of David and formed a northern alliance under their new king, Jeroboam. Henceforth the tribes were divided into the northern kingdom of Israel and the southern kingdom of Judah. The two kingdoms would go their own separate ways, sometimes warring against each other, sometimes warring side by side, until the northern kingdom was carried away into exile by the Assyrians in 722 BC. The southern kingdom would continue for another one hundred and fifty years or so, until they also were carried away into exile by the Babylonians in 586 BC.

The northern kingdom under Jeroboam soon fell into idolatry by erecting rival shrines in the north. King Jeroboam set up these rival shrines because he recognized the importance of the Ark and its cultus for all Israel. He correctly discerned that it would be difficult to create political unity within his ten northern tribes if they kept going south to worship at the original shrine in Jerusalem, for it was the old center of political unity. Jeroboam therefore took the disastrous step of setting up rival shrines within his own northern tribal boundaries, so that the northern tribes might go there rather than to Jerusalem. It was a shrewd move politically, but a catastrophic one spiritually, for it meant defying Yahweh and institutionalizing idolatry.

It was during these times of apostasy that God raised up Elijah. The king reigning over the northern kingdom in his days favored a policy of religious syncretism, one that combined the ancestral worship of Yahweh with the worship of Baal, an old Canaanite fertility deity. The policy was applauded by many in Israel as cosmopolitan enlightenment, the inevitable result of having left a life of wandering in the desert for a settled life in a fertile land. The prophets of Yahweh denounced it as idolatry, betrayal of Yahweh's covenant, and a quick road to disaster. They also denounced the king promoting the policy, resulting in tension between the royal house and the prophets of Yahweh, with the former doing all it could to exterminate the latter (compare 1 Kin. 18:13; 19:10).

The historical books record the words and deeds of Elijah, as well as of his successor Elisha. The text puts great stress on their miracles, to show that the God who miraculously brought Israel out of Egypt—and who therefore could give military victory—was not Baal, but Yahweh, whose pure worship was preserved by Elijah and Elisha. Their miracles were not recorded for hagiographical entertainment, but to reveal who the true and saving God really was. The miraculous God of the Exodus was alive and well in Israel and dwelt far from the royal shrines, in the midst of the prophets, the holy remnant that kept faith with Yahweh when the rest of the kingdom had gone astray.

We shall look at two of these miracles, for these have special resonance for Christians. One is the contest of Elijah on Mount Carmel, found in 1 Kings 18.

It was an uneven contest, humanly speaking. On the one side stood four hundred and fifty prophets of Baal, and another four hundred prophets of Baal's consort, Asherah, all of them in the royal employ. On the other side stood Elijah, the lone prophet of Yahweh, hunted by King Ahab and Queen Jezebel. A great multitude watched the contest. Elijah put a challenge before them: Let the worshippers of Baal choose one of two available bulls, cut it in pieces, and lay it on the wood of an altar, but put no fire to it. Elijah would do likewise with the other bull. Each would call upon their deity to send fire from heaven to consume the sacrifice, and all would acknowledge the deity who answered with fire as the true God. The other deity would be spurned as an idol, a snare for Israel, and its worship would be regarded as a capital offense. The people agreed.

The prophets of Baal were invited to go first. They called on Baal loudly from morning to noon. At noon, Elijah mocked their efforts. "Call louder, since he is a god! Maybe he is preoccupied or on the toilet [literally, "turned aside"], or away on a trip, or has dozed off!" (1 Kin. 18:27 NASB). These were shocking impieties, and intended to be so. Elijah heaped them on the mighty Baal to show that Baal was nothing and was incapable of proving or avenging himself.

When the prophets of Baal fell down exhausted and acknowledged defeat, it was Elijah's turn. He repaired an altar, deliberately using twelve stones in memorial of Yahweh's ancient covenant with all twelve tribes (vv. 30–31). He dug a trench around the altar and put the wood on it, then put on the sacrifice. Then he did something unusual. He ordered the people to pour on water, soaking the sacrifice and the wood. He ordered them to do it a second time, and a third. Only then, when he had weighted the contest against himself and soaked the sacrifice with water so that it filled the surrounding trench, did he call on Yahweh.

The response was immediate and vigorous. "Then the fire of the LORD fell and consumed the burnt sacrifice, and the wood and the stones and the dust, and it licked up the water that *was* in the trench" (v. 38). The people fell on their faces, confessing with fear that Yahweh was indeed the true God, saying, "The LORD, He *is* God! The LORD, He *is* God!" (v. 39). The day belonged to Yahweh and His prophet Elijah.

For us who have experienced a triple soaking as the sign of belonging to the God of Elijah, the story has special import. In an apostate world, we confess the one true God who manifested Himself in His Son, Jesus Christ. As with Elijah, this faithfulness brings many foes who seek to persecute us. As a sign of allegiance to God, we are soaked three times (whether by immersion or pouring), and after this, the Pentecostal fire falls from heaven on our souls. The Lord said that He had come to kindle this fire on the earth (Luke 12:49), and we experience this baptism of fire ourselves (Luke 3:16). And as Elijah offered a sacrifice to Yahweh on the altar, so we offer ourselves as living sacrifices to God (Rom. 12:1).

Baptized in water and having received the heavenly fire, we look at the contest on Mount Carmel as prefiguring our own experience of faithfulness to God. And like the children of Israel who stood watching this dramatic contest, we must choose every day whom we will serve—either the Lord Jesus or the spirit of the age. The choice is stark and unavoidable. The water and fire of Elijah compel us to confess that "the LORD, He is God!" and to accept no other Lord but Jesus.

Another miracle that has special resonance for us is the cleansing of Naaman the Syrian at the hands of Elisha, recorded in 2 Kings 5. The prophet Elisha, as Elijah's commissioned successor, also spoke and worked miracles during days of apostasy and crisis. In those days there was international tension between the kingdom of Israel and the nation

The Historical Books

of Syria (literally, "Aram") to the north. One of the maids of Israel had been carried off to Syria in a border raid, and she worked as slave for Naaman, a commander in the Syrian army who suffered from leprosy. She knew of Elisha's reputation as a wonderworker and boasted to her mistress (in a bit of thoughtless patriotism) that Elisha could surely heal her master. Accordingly, the king of Syria sent a letter to the king of Israel, stating his determination to send Naaman to him so that he could be healed of his leprosy. An appropriately tremendous gift of gold, silver, and festal garments attended the letter. The king of Israel could hardly refuse without creating an international incident.

The king was beside himself, considering this a transparent provocation and an excuse for Syria to go to war. But when Elisha heard of this impending threat to peace, he encouraged the king to send the leper to him. "Please let him come to me, and he shall know that there is a prophet in Israel" (2 Kin. 5:8).

Naaman at length arrived with a great retinue, turning up at the door of Elisha's house. The prophet greeted him with what the great general considered offensive casualness. He didn't even come out to welcome him (a great breach of Middle Eastern hospitality), but simply sent a message saying, "Go and wash in the Jordan seven times, and your flesh shall be restored to you, and *you shall* be clean" (2 Kin. 5:10). It was nine words in the original Hebrew.

Naaman was *not* impressed. "Indeed, I said to myself, 'He will surely come out *to me*, and stand and call on the name of the LORD his God, and wave his hand over the place, and heal the leprosy.' *Are* not the Abanah and the Pharpar, the rivers of Damascus, better than all the waters of Israel? Could I not wash in them and be clean?" (2 Kin. 5:11–12). He was furious and stormed away to mount his chariot to ride out of there for home. He felt slighted by the prophet, who seemed to be saying that Israelite waters alone would do the trick, as if Israel was that much better than Syria. After the long hot trip from Syria, it appeared that the much-vaunted prophet was nothing more than a nationalistic jingo.

Naaman's aide, however, recalled him to a place of humility. "My father," he implored, "*if* the prophet had told you *to do* something great, would you not have done *it*? How much more then, when he says to you, 'Wash, and be clean'?" (2 Kin. 5:13). Chastened (and perhaps thinking he had nothing to lose), Naaman the leper went down to the Jordan and immersed himself as commanded, "and his flesh was restored like the flesh of a little child, and he was clean" (2 Kin. 5:14). There was indeed a God in Israel, and the healing of this foreigner proved that He was God over all the earth. His mercy to a foreign Gentile revealed His universal power and His love.

Like the story of Elijah on Mount Carmel, the story of the dipping of Naaman in the Jordan could hardly fail to attract the special notice of us who were dipped in baptism, recalling the Master's dipping in that same Jordan. Immersions in obedience to the word of God's prophet cleansed the foreigner of the disease of leprosy. Corresponding to this, immersions in obedience to the word of God's Son cleanse us of the leprosy of sin. Cleansing the foreign Gentile was a sign that God's power and love covered the whole world. The parallel with baptism is unmistakable and cannot have been accidental. This is not coincidence, but prophecy. The same God who healed us of our inner uncleanness through immersion foreshadowed this sacramental cleansing through the immersion of Naaman. And as Naaman could only find healing through humbly accepting the word of Yahweh's prophet, so we can only find salvation through humility. In pride Naaman almost lost the opportunity to be healed of his disease; it was only at the last moment that his aide called him to repent humbly of his pride. We also must embrace humility and submit to the Word of God's Christ if we are to abide in spiritual health.

It was also not accidental that both Elijah and Elisha did miracles that typified Christian baptism. Both of these prophets were prophets of the remnant, serving God in days of persecution and difficulty. Their light shone all the brighter since it shone in the midst of such darkness. We serve God in such days as well, and what brings us from the darkness of paganism to the light of the God of the prophets is the sacrament of baptism. It is not surprising to find that sacrament prominent in the lives of our prophetic forefathers.

The Message of History

Throughout the historical books of the Old Testament, we see something new and unique in the ancient world—a God who works openly in history on the world stage, leaving His footprints in the sacred history of Israel and in the pages of secular records. He entered into dialogue with Israel's kings, blessing and rebuking them, saving and judging them, as their deeds deserved. He gave His Word to His prophets, and these prophets worked with kings and commoners, sometimes supporting the kings and sometimes suffering under them.

The historical books record God's doings and His desire to interact with the men and women He created. As the Lord of every nation under heaven, He used all the nations to fulfill His holy purposes. His hand could be felt in Egypt, in Moab, in Edom, in Syria, in Babylon, in Persia—and in His own Holy Land. Later secular historians recorded what were, in reality, the judgments of God.

In this, Yahweh differed from all the other gods. Those gods and goddesses were essentially personifications of the forces of nature, fertility deities. Invoked by their worshippers, they worked primarily through the powers of nature, in the ceaseless annual cycle of rain and growth and harvest. Sometimes they could be persuaded to give their devotees victory in battle (see Judg. 11:24), but their power and jurisdiction were local and limited. Their power was not primarily seen on the international stage, but in the cycles of nature, in the death of the land in winter and its rebirth in the spring. It was as if they did not (or could not) aspire to greater works than providing agricultural prosperity.

Yahweh was different. He was not just sovereign over nature. As the Creator of the natural world, of course He was its Master. But He was sovereign over history too, working in all the earth through the historical process. As He proclaimed through the prophet Amos, "Did I not bring up Israel from the land of Egypt, / The Philistines from Caphtor, / And the Syrians from Kir?" (Amos 9:7). Yahweh was the ultimate author of all that transpired under the sun, and the victories and defeats of Philistines, Syrians, Babylonians, Persians, and every other tribe and people came from Him. Unlike the other gods worshipped by these nations, the God of Israel was the Lord of history. And as its Lord, He was directing history to a specific goal. That goal was recorded by some of the prophets. They called it "the Day of the Lord." The Church knows it by the name, "the Kingdom of God."

CHAPTER 4

THE PROPHETS: LISTENING TO GOD

Prophecy within Israel

THE INSTITUTION OF PROPHECY had a long and varied history in Israel. It is rooted in Israel's desire on Mount Sinai to hear a mediated word from God, rather than to hear His unmediated voice direct from the mountaintop. God spoke to His people from Mount Sinai amid "the thunderings, the lightning flashes, the sound of the trumpet, and the mountain smoking; and when the people saw *it*, they trembled." They stood at a distance and besought Moses, "You speak with us, and we will hear; but let not God speak with us, lest we die" (Ex. 20:18–19). God approved of this request, and thereafter spoke His Word to them through human intermediaries, such as Moses.

As Moses said in Deuteronomy 18:15–18:

> "The LORD your God will raise up for you a Prophet like me from your midst, from your brethren. Him you shall hear, according to all you desired of the LORD your God in Horeb in the day of the assembly, saying, 'Let me not hear again the voice of the LORD my God, nor let me see this great fire anymore, lest I die.' "And the LORD said to me: 'What they have spoken is good. I will raise up for them a Prophet like you from among their brethren, and will put My words in His mouth, and He shall speak to them all that I command Him.'"

The institution of prophecy—that is, of a human being carrying the divine Word—finds its ultimate expression in the Incarnation. The Church was not wrong in following the exegesis that saw in Moses' promise of another "Prophet like me" a prophecy of Christ. Nonetheless, this passage is not primarily predicting the coming of a certain prophetic individual, but establishing the office of prophet *per se*. The institution of prophecy is Mosaic. God desired not only to give Israel His Law once and for all, but also to enter into a constant dialogue of exhortation and response with His people. He would dwell among them through both the Tabernacle and the prophets.

Samuel was an early example of such a prophet (the term in his day was "a seer"; compare 1 Sam. 9:9). He received revelations from God and would speak them authoritatively in Yahweh's Name. The prophets in his day tended to work as roving bands, speaking oracles in response to wild music (see 1 Sam. 10:5). The oracles tended to be ecstatic, so that the speaker temporarily lost control of his faculties—as happened to Saul when the prophetic spirit came upon him (1 Sam. 10:10; 19:20–24). Indeed, the verb "to prophesy"—Hebrew *naba*—is also the verb "to rave" (compare 1 Sam. 10:6 and 18:10 NASB).

During the monarchy, prophets were attached to the royal house, usually as supporters of royal policy. Thus Ahab king of Israel had four hundred prophets on his payroll, who could be counted on to support his policy and offer assurances of divine approval (see 1 Kin. 22:5–6). Thus Zedekiah king of Judah had the prophet Hananiah, a prophet from Gibeon, who could be counted upon to support the royal policy of resistance against Babylon (Jer. 28:1–4). But obviously all prophets were not such time-serving hirelings. Micaiah stood alone against King Ahab's wishes and prophesied disaster if the king followed his desired policy—and paid the price of keeping integrity in difficult times (1 Kin. 22:7–28). Jeremiah too prophesied unpopular things to King Zedekiah, and also paid the price (Jer. 27:12–22; 37:15).

Most prophets left no literary legacy. But some of them did, and their disciples and fellow prophets collected their written oracles and preserved them. These are the works of the biblical prophets such as Isaiah, Jeremiah, Amos, Micah, Hosea, and Joel. They served God in a variety of political situations, sometimes enjoying royal support, sometimes enduring royal persecution. All of them called the people back to the covenant God made with them through Moses on Mount Sinai, promising blessing in return for repentance and obedience, and judgment in return for hardness of heart and disobedience. Though there were examples of royal obedience (King Hezekiah and King Josiah come to mind), the people largely rejected the words of the prophets denouncing idolatry and social injustice.

In examining the prophetic words preserved in the Old Testament, it is important to locate them in the cultural and political context of their times. Their words were not like the pretended oracles of Nostradamus—predictions of supposed actual future events, inviting hearers to combine prophecy with fulfillment in a kind of one-to-one correspondence. Prophecy is not simple prediction, "history written in advance" as some have said. Prophecy is divine poetry, revealing what God loves and what He hates, holding out rewards for conformity with the former and judgment for conformity with the latter. Disaster can be promised, but yet still avoided, if the hearers will repent and embrace what God loves and commands.

A prominent example of this is the apparently unconditional prophecy of Jonah. In the story, Jonah declared to Nineveh, "Yet forty days, and Nineveh shall be overthrown!" (Jonah 3:4). There was no room left for ambiguity—the doom seemed as sure as that pronounced in the Book of Nahum concerning Nineveh: "Woe to the bloody city! / It *is* all full of lies *and* robbery. / *Its* victim never departs. . . . All who hear news of you / Will clap *their* hands over you, / For upon whom has not your wickedness passed continually?" (Nahum 3:1, 19). Yet despite the certainty of Jonah's word, God did not overthrow Nineveh in forty days, since those in the city repented.

This is characteristic of all prophecy. The prophets did not just foretell the future: they also offered a choice of futures. Which future occurred depended entirely upon the people receiving the prophetic Word. The task of the prophets was to speak God's part in the dialogue He initiated with His covenant people. "Come, let us reason together," is the cry not just of Isaiah (Is. 1:18), but of all the prophets. God's intention in sending prophets was not to reveal destiny, but to offer life instead of death. All the prophetic poetry, imagery, metaphor, parable, drama, and symbol had Israel's repentance and blessing as its final goal. It is true that the prophets foretold a coming salvation and Kingdom, which was certain, whatever the choices of men. But this foretold salvation must be located in the ongoing dialogue of God with His people, in which He took their choices seriously and responded accordingly.

In the following sections, we will examine a handful of the many prophecies preserved in the Old Testament texts. Many are from the prophet Isaiah, whose canonical Book has been called "the fifth Gospel," since it so clearly and often reveals Jesus Christ. In these texts, we will see some of the rich variety of literary forms the prophets used as they strove to make their blind and deaf audience see and hear the Word of God, which alone could save them.

The Immanuel Oracles: Isaiah 7—8

As recorded in Isaiah 7, in about the year 735 BC, King Ahaz and the southern kingdom of Judah were facing annihilation. They were menaced by a coalition from the north, consisting of Rezin king of Syria and Pekah king of Israel. Expecting a long siege, King Ahaz was checking out the water supply at the end of the conduit of the upper pool. He was planning to appeal to the superpower Assyria for help, making a covenant with them in exchange for his loyalty. (Such covenants inevitably involved acceptance of their gods as well.)

Isaiah saw the folly in such shortsighted remedies and met the king in the field to encourage him to trust in Yahweh's help, rather than in the might of Assyria. The prophet took his son Shear-jashub with him. The boy's name meant "A remnant will return," and doubtless Isaiah thought his very name would provide hope to strengthen the king's resolve to trust in Yahweh alone. The prophet had a message for his king: Do not be afraid of this present threat, for God will bring it to nothing. He invited the king to ask for a sign in confirmation of God's promise and not to give in to the temptation to put his hope in Assyria.

King Ahaz would have none of it. He was determined to call in the

The Prophets

Assyrians, and he therefore put off Isaiah, refusing his offer of a sign under the pious pretext of not putting Yahweh to the test. Then Isaiah proclaimed the word of the Lord:

> "Hear now, O house of David! *Is it* a small thing for you to weary men, but will you weary my God also? Therefore the Lord Himself will give you a sign: Behold, the virgin shall conceive and bear a Son, and shall call His name Immanuel. . . . For before the Child shall know to refuse the evil and choose the good, the land that you dread will be forsaken by both her kings." (Is. 7:13–16)

Furthermore, Isaiah went on to say, the judgment will come from the very king of Assyria whose help you invoked.

There was more. As recorded in Isaiah 8, Isaiah took witnesses trusted by all and had them watch while he wrote on a large placard a name, "Maher-shalal-hash-baz"—which meant "Quick loot, fast plunder"—a reference to the coming invasion by Assyria. He later approached his wife and she conceived and bore a son, whom Isaiah named Maher-shalal-hash-baz, the name written on the placard (Is. 8:1–3). In this way, all would know that Isaiah had prophesied the speedy destruction and looting of Syria and Israel by the Assyrians. The fact that the boy was named for the event well before its occurrence proved the truth of Isaiah's prophecy. Isaiah assured everyone that "before the child shall have knowledge to cry 'My father' and 'My mother,' the riches of Damascus and the spoil of Samaria will be taken away before the king of Assyria" (Is. 8:4).

Isaiah further prophesied that the king of Assyria would come as a mighty flood, sweeping away not only Syria and Israel, but Judah as well, the "land of Immanuel." The peoples of the nations might devise whatever plans they wished, but only the Lord's plan would stand, for *emmanu El*—in Hebrew, "God is with us" (Is. 8:8–10).

These, in brief, are the beginnings of the Immanuel oracles. What do they mean?

A key to understanding this oracle is the recognition that the "sign" offered King Ahaz was not the miraculous nature of the birth of Immanuel, but its timing. That is, before the boy knew enough to refuse bad food and choose good, the menacing lands of Syria and Israel would be forsaken (7:16). Children at the breast know nothing about solid food, but toddlers soon learn what food is pleasant and what food is unpleasant. Therefore the devastation of Syria and Israel would occur within two or three years—the length of time needed for a woman to conceive, bear a child, and have that child know enough about food to be fussy. This interpretation is confirmed by Isaiah's further word in 8:4: before his own son, named in advance "Quick loot, fast plunder," was able to articulate the words *abbi* and *immi* (i.e. papa, mama), the looting and plundering for which he was named would be over. But this looting and plundering of Syria and Israel was not all good news, for Assyria would come to loot and plunder them too, flooding Judah (here called "the land of Immanuel").

Who then was this Immanuel for whom Judah was to be named in the next few years? It is clear that Jesus of Nazareth cannot be the primary fulfillment, for these words were spoken in about 735 BC, and Christ's birth over seven centuries later could hardly have any urgent chronological significance for those in the eighth century BC. Also, there must be some connection between the birth of Immanuel and the birth of Maher-shalal-hash-baz, for the chronological marker of an early toddler's progress is common to both.

I suggest that the "virgin" who was to conceive and bear a son whom she would name Immanuel was the average virgin of Judah in that day. The word translated as "virgin" is the Hebrew *almah*, meaning any young woman of marriageable age. (The Greek translates it as *parthenos*.) The word *almah* appears in Genesis 24:43, describing Rebekah, and in Psalm 68:25, where it describes ordinary young girls. The emphasis is not on their sexual inexperience, but their young age (although doubtless a respectable *almah* would also be physically virginal).

Isaiah's point is that young maidens in Judah then engaged would get married, conceive (in the usual way), bear children, and by the time these babies were old enough to begin to be fussy about food, the crisis would be over. God would soon deliver Judah, and this deliverance would be reflected in the names given to these babies soon to be conceived. The prophet's wife and new son were offered as an example: the boy's name reflected events soon to occur, though in the prophet Isaiah's case, the name was chosen *before* the birth as a proof of the prophecy. All the names were not necessarily Immanuel—"God is with us." Isaiah's boy, for example, was named Maher-shalal-hash-baz. But all the names reflected the theme that God was with them. So many babies would be born referring to this deliverance that Judah could be thought of as the "land of Immanuel."

Why then have we Christians always proclaimed that this prophecy was fulfilled in Jesus? It was not because Jews expected the Messiah would be born from a physically virginal woman. When Matthew wrote that the virgin birth of Christ took place to fulfill the Immanuel prophecy (Matt. 1:22–23), he was not writing this in order to conform to contemporary Jewish expectation, since the Jews had no such expectation. But since he knew the facts of Jesus' virginal conception from the Theotokos (who was, after all, a part of the Christian community in Jerusalem), he could not have failed to be struck by the verbal coincidence in the text of Isaiah. The prophecy said that in a time of apostasy, God would move definitively to save His people and show that He was among them, and the sign of this saving presence would be the birth of a son from a *parthenos*. The situation fit exactly with that of Jesus' birth.

This astonishing example of verbal coincidence with the life of Jesus is found elsewhere in the writings of the prophets. In Hosea 11:1, for example, God encourages His people, saying, "When Israel was a child, I loved him, and out of Egypt I called My son [Gr. *uios*]."[4] The passage is not referring to the Messiah, but to the people of Israel, for it goes on to say, "The more I called them, the more they went from Me; they kept sacrificing to the Baals" (Hosea 11:2 NASB). That is, God called Israel His son, but they continued to refuse His call even from the days of Egypt. Yet Matthew, knowing that Jesus did in fact sojourn in Egypt during His childhood and was called from there back to Palestine (Matt. 2:13–15), was struck by the verbal coincidence of God's "son" being called out of

---

4   Those who insist that "the Septuagint was the Bible of the apostles" may wish to know that the Septuagint does not have this reading, but rather, "Israel was an infant and I loved him, and out of Egypt I recalled his children [Gr. *tekna*]." St. Matthew here cites the Hebrew, not the Septuagint. It would be more accurate to state that the Septuagint was a major resource for the apostles.

Egypt. Here was a coincidence that was more providentially prophetic than it was coincidental. It was the same for the sign of Immanuel being born from a *parthenos*—it also was providentially prophetic.

That the sign of Immanuel born from a *parthenos* was divinely intended to have typological and messianic significance can be seen from the wider context as well. In the Immanuel oracles, the text begins with the current crisis with Syria and Israel in chapters 7—8, and then in chapter 9 opens up into a new and larger vista, as the eighth century BC begins to coalesce with the more distant future, a bright glimpse of the messianic Kingdom. The Immanuel oracles, therefore, were not only about a passing crisis of the eighth century, but also about the Messiah—as St. Matthew recognized.

The Immanuel Oracles: Isaiah 9

In the latter part of the oracles recorded beginning in chapter 9, those coming bright days of the Messiah are contrasted with the darkness found by the apostates who rejected Isaiah's word. The apostates "will look to the earth, and see trouble and darkness, gloom of anguish; and *they will be* driven into darkness." The passage continues:

> Nevertheless the gloom *will* not *be* upon her who *is* distressed,
> As when at first He lightly esteemed
> The land of Zebulun and the land of Naphtali,
> And afterward more heavily oppressed *her,*
> *By* the way of the sea, beyond the Jordan,
> In Galilee of the Gentiles.
> The people who walked in darkness
> Have seen a great light;
> Those who dwelt in the land of the shadow of death,
> Upon them a light has shined.
> ...
> For unto us a Child is born,
> Unto us a Son is given;
> And the government will be upon His shoulder.

> And His name will be called
> Wonderful, Counselor, Mighty God,
> Everlasting Father, Prince of Peace.[5] (Is. 8:22—9:2, 6)

In this messianic prophecy, Isaiah speaks of the darkness of those northern tribes who sat in anguish, expecting the judgment of invasion, which always came from the north. But no more. Soon a son would be born who would take away the darkness. The northern tribes could relax and live in the light of peace and security. This child, given as the gift of God, would have miraculous counsel for Israel; He would manifest the mighty heroic power of God Himself. He would be a father and protector to his people, a prince who would bestow peace and prosperity (Heb. *shalom*).

Like the name Immanuel, the name Pele-Yuets-El-Gibbor-Abi-Ad-Sar-Shalom is not so much an individual's given name as a revelation of what the son given by God to His people would do for them. Isaiah was not saying that the Messiah's actual name would be Immanuel or Pele-Yuets-El-Gibbor-Abi-Ad-Sar-Shalom. (The actual name, as it turned out, was Yeshua, Joshua, Jesus.) Isaiah was not recording names for future archives, like some sort of scribal statistician. He was writing poetry, exulting in the change of fortunes this messianic child would bring. The name by which men would call this child revealed what he would mean to them. Let us look at the different parts of the name, one by one.

The child would be called "Wonderful Counselor." "Wonderful" here means "causing wonder, amazement" (compare its usage in Ps. 139:6, where the psalmist confesses that God's knowledge is too "wonderful" for him to comprehend). The counsel and wisdom offered by this king would be so deep that men would be astonished by it.

The child would be called "Mighty God." The word here rendered "mighty" is the Hebrew *gibbor*, elsewhere rendered "mighty one," and applied to the mighty men of valor, the warriors who served King David (e.g. 1 Chr. 11:19). The word often has a military or athletic ring to it.

---

5   The name in Hebrew is "Pele-Yuets-El-Gibbor-Abi-Ad-Sar-Shalom." (The Greek Septuagint simply says, "His name will be called "Messenger [or Angel] of Great Counsel.")

The king will be a valiant soldier, having all the might and prowess of God Himself to wage war and defend his people.

The child would called be "Everlasting Father." In Hebrew thought, a father is not simply a biological progenitor, but one who offers life, support, and protection (compare 2 Sam. 7:14; Ps. 89:26). The king's paternal protection would be called "everlasting" because the life and protection he would offer would be everlasting, unfailing, unfading (Heb. *olam*).

He would be called "Prince of Peace." The word rendered "peace" is the Hebrew *shalom*, denoting not simply the absence of war, but abundance, prosperity, fullness. In the Kingdom, God promises He will "extend *shalom* to [Jerusalem] like a river, and the wealth of the nations like an overflowing stream" (Is. 66:12 NASB). Note that in the poetic parallelism of this verse, "peace"/*shalom* is parallel with "the wealth of the nations." It is this abundance that the king would provide for his people.

Some later Jewish exegesis would suggest that these prophecies were fulfilled in King Hezekiah. Hezekiah was a good and righteous king, but he cannot measure up to the glowing picture of this future king presented here. Surveying the long and checkered history of Israel and then looking to our own Lord Jesus, we assert that this prophecy is fulfilled only in Him.

The king was to be called "Wonderful Counselor," having a depth of wisdom which amazed his hearers. "And so it was, when Jesus had ended these sayings, that the people were astonished at His teaching" (Matt. 7:28). When the officers sent to arrest Jesus came back empty-handed, they explained themselves by saying, "No one ever spoke like this Man!" (John 7:46).

The king was to be called "Mighty God." We see this divine might in Jesus as He overcomes the strong man, Satan, casting out demons and setting men free (Mark 3:27). This might will be revealed to all at the end of the age: "Now I saw heaven opened, and behold, a white horse. And He who sat on him *was* called Faithful and True, and in righteousness He judges and makes war" (Rev. 19:11).

The king was to be called "Everlasting Father" because he would offer life and protection to his people. Jesus offers this life and protection to His disciples: "If anyone enters by Me, he will be saved, and will go in and out and find pasture. . . . And I give them eternal life, and they shall never perish; neither shall anyone snatch them out of My hand" (John 10:9, 28).

The king was to be called "Prince of Peace" because in his reign abundance would flourish. Christ offers this spiritual abundance and peace with God. As He said, "I have come that they may have life, and that they may have *it* more abundantly" (John 10:10).

The realities reflected in the prophetic name Pele-Yuets-El-Gibbor-Abi-Ad-Sar-Shalom find their fulfillment in Jesus of Nazareth alone.

The Immanuel Oracles: Isaiah 10—12

The Immanuel collection of oracles continues with Isaiah 10, pronouncing divine judgment through the invading Assyrians. Judah will be judged, like a fruitful forest being burned up by a raging forest fire. "Then the rest of the trees of his forest / Will be so few in number / That a child may write them" (Is. 10:19). Yet after this, "a remnant shall return" (Heb. *shear jashub*, the name of Isaiah's son mentioned in 7:3). God will restore His people, turning His judgment instead upon Assyria, which struck them. And then, after promising justice, Isaiah proclaims good news for Israel.

> There shall come forth a Rod [Heb. *netzer*] from the stem
>   of Jesse,
> And a Branch shall grow out of his roots.
> The Spirit of the LORD shall rest upon Him,
> The Spirit of wisdom and understanding,
> The Spirit of counsel and might,
> The Spirit of knowledge and of the fear of the LORD.
> . . .
> And He shall not judge by the sight of His eyes,
> Nor decide by the hearing of His ears;
> But with righteousness He shall judge the poor . . .
> He shall strike the earth with the rod of His mouth,
> And with the breath of His lips He shall slay the wicked.
> . . .

> The wolf also shall dwell with the lamb,
> The leopard shall lie down with the young goat.
> ...
> They shall not hurt nor destroy in all My holy mountain,
> For the earth shall be full of the knowledge of the LORD
> As the waters cover the sea.
> And in that day there shall be a Root of Jesse,
> Who shall stand as a banner to the people;
> For the Gentiles shall seek Him,
> And His resting place shall be glorious.
> ...
> And in that day you will say:
> "O LORD, I will praise You;
> Though You were angry with me,
> Your anger is turned away, and You comfort me. . . .
> 'For YAH, the LORD, *is* my strength and song;
> He also has become my salvation.'" (Is. 11:1–10; 12:1–2)

With these words of hope, the prophet once more leaves the prosaic world of his own day and looks ahead with poetic heart to the coming Kingdom. This description fits no king who ever sat on the historical throne of Judah, but like the description of the son given to God's people in Isaiah 9:2–7, applies to the Messiah.

The coming Messiah will be "a Rod from the stem of Jesse," "a Branch . . . out of his roots." In the impending judgment, all the tall trees (the proud kings of the day) would be chopped down, and those left standing would be so few that "a child may write them" (Is. 10:19). Most of the trees felled by God would never grow again, but not the tree of the House of David, with whom God had made an undying covenant. From that felled tree, a shoot would spring and a branch from its roots would bear fruit. It would be but a small, sprouting twig, but it would hold the promise of great future growth.

This theme of the felled stump of the House of David sprouting again is found in other writings of the prophets. Jeremiah prophesied the rebirth of David's House: "'Behold, *the* days are coming,' says the LORD, / 'That I will raise to David a Branch [Heb. *semeh*] of righteousness; / A

King shall reign and prosper, / And execute judgment and righteousness in the earth'" (Jer. 23:5). Zechariah prophesied the same: "Behold, I am bringing forth My Servant the BRANCH [Heb. *semeh*]" (Zech. 3:8). The words used to describe this twig are different (Isaiah using *netzer* and Jeremiah and Zechariah using *semeh*), but the thought is the same: From the felled stump of David's royal house, a humble sprout would spring up and survive. The Messiah would come and Israel would again bear fruit.

Unlike the House of David in Isaiah's day, craven and morally compromised, the messianic Son of David would be righteous, for the Spirit of God would rest upon him, giving him wisdom and understanding, making him strong and wise. Unlike those kings who reserved their highest fear for the foreign kings of the earth and relied on them, the Messiah would look only to Yahweh his God. He would dispense true justice to his people, not relying on external testimony of eyes and ears when he judged for the poor, but upon supernatural wisdom from God. The wicked who controlled the land in the time of Ahaz and embittered the lives of the helpless poor would finally be condemned and put down from their thrones,[6] for he would issue sure commands for their destruction, striking the earth with the rod of his mouth, slaying the wicked with the breath of his lips. In his time, righteousness would flourish, and peace would reign. The ravening wolf would dwell with the lamb as oppression and crime ceased from the land.

This blessing of peace would not be confined to Israel. The Messiah's influence would be felt by all, so that the whole earth would be full of the knowledge of the Lord as the waters cover the sea. For all the nations would resort to the root of Jesse and seek his wisdom. God's power would be upon him, so that his resting place in Zion would be full of divine glory. Through this king, God would act to save His people. The anger of past devastation and exile would be forgotten as God would now comfort and rebuild His people. Israel would confess with joy that He had come and saved them.

As with the picture of the king presented in Isaiah 9:2–7, we find this description fits none other than our own Lord Jesus. He is the One upon whom rests the Spirit of Yahweh. As John said, though others

---

6   Compare Luke 1:52.

receive a measure of the Spirit of God, it is Jesus to whom "He gives the Spirit without measure" (John 3:34 NASB). The Spirit rested upon Him when He was baptized by the Forerunner in the River Jordan, and having been anointed with the Spirit and power, He went about doing good and healing all who were oppressed by the devil (Acts 10:38).

The work of the king in this prophecy, vindicating the poor and striking down their oppressors, finds final and superlative expression in the work of Jesus, who lifted the burdens from the lives of those who formerly had no hope and set them free, striking down Satan and freeing them from his grip. It is in His Kingdom that the wolf dwells with the lamb, the terrorizing Zealot with the collaborating tax-collector (see Luke 6:15), and former enemies embrace one another in forgiveness. In His Kingdom alone is the dividing wall of ancient hostility torn down, so that Jew and Gentile exchange the kiss of peace and drink from the same saving chalice (Eph. 2:14–15).

It is through Him alone that this Kingdom of peace and the word of reconciliation have gone out into the whole world, so that all the earth is full of the knowledge of the Lord as the waters cover the sea. Nations that once were far from God and His righteousness now resort to the root of Jesse, Jesus Christ, who stands as God's beacon of light, drawing all the people of the world to Him. All God's people, Jew and Gentile alike, would confess that God's anger at their sin had been replaced with forgiveness (Eph. 2:3–7). Standing before Him through Jesus Christ, they would exult that God had become their salvation.

Meditating on the Hebrew of this messianic prophecy, we find something more. Isaiah, like the prophets Jeremiah and Zechariah, declared that the Messiah would arise from humble beginnings, like a little branching twig growing from an old felled stump. The Hebrew of the word "rod" in this prophecy is *netzer*. Christians have always been challenged about the humble beginnings of Jesus—a mere carpenter, unconnected with the glorious ones of the earth, having no place to lay His head. His family was known, and people thought them nothing special (Mark 6:1–3). And He came from Nazareth!—a humble village, far from the centers of power, a village of which one could ask, "Can anything good come out of Nazareth?" (John 1:46).

Christian interpretation saw the humility of Christ's beginnings reflected in the word *netzer*, for just as the king came from a humble *netzer*, so Jesus came from humble Nazareth—the consonants of both words are the same. Such wordplays were common in the Scriptures in Hebrew, a consonantal language. For example, see the many wordplays of Micah 1:10, such as, "At Beth-le-aphrah ['house of dust'], roll in the dust . . . the inhabitant of Zaanan ['going out'] does not go out." Micah sees hidden and ominous significance in the names of the towns in the path of invasion. Puns were part of the scriptural tradition.

St. Matthew wrote from within a venerable tradition when he found in the word *netzer* a foreshadowing of the fact that Jesus would be called a Nazarene (Matt. 2:23).

Israel as a Third with Assyria and Egypt: Isaiah 19:18–25

One of the most astonishing prophecies of the entire Old Testament is found in the last verses of Isaiah 19. Israel looked upon Egypt and Assyria as its two greatest national foes, as the quintessence of all God had taught them to despise. Yet this oracle in chapter 19 reverses these thoughts. It speaks of these foes as being God's covenant people equally with Israel.

> In that day five cities in the land of Egypt will speak the language of Canaan and swear by the LORD of hosts . . . In that day there will be an altar to the LORD in the midst of the land of Egypt, and a pillar to the LORD at its border. And it will be for a sign and for a witness to the LORD of hosts in the land of Egypt; for they will cry to the LORD because of the oppressors, and He will send them a Savior and a Mighty One, and He will deliver them. Then the LORD will be known to Egypt, and the Egyptians will know the LORD in that day, and will make sacrifice and offering; yes, they will make a vow to the LORD and perform it. . . . In that day there will be a highway from Egypt to Assyria, and the Assyrian will come into Egypt and the Egyptian into Assyria, and the Egyptians will serve with the Assyrians. In that day Israel will be one of three with Egypt and Assyria—a blessing in the midst of the land, whom the LORD of hosts shall bless,

saying, "Blessed *is* Egypt My people, and Assyria the work of My hands, and Israel My inheritance." (Is. 19:18–25)

We find it difficult, imbued as we are with a spirit of internationalism and the idea that all are equal before God, to feel the original force of these words as they struck the hearts of their first hearers. These words stand on its head the whole spiritual and psychological world of Isaiah's day. They take all the vocabulary of covenant salvation—images of an altar for sacrifice and a memorial pillar (compare Deut. 12:5ff; 1 Sam. 7:12); of crying to God for help and Him sending saviors and champions (compare Judges 2:16ff); of making vows to elicit God's help and keeping them once God had delivered them (compare Ps. 50:14–15)—and apply these to God's ancestral and current enemies. These scandalous words seem to suggest that Yahweh would deal with Israel's sworn enemies in exactly the same way and with the same covenant faithfulness with which He dealt with Israel.

Despite the Egyptians and the Assyrians having different gods, the oracle envisions these two nations joining together in worshipping the one God, the God of the Hebrews. This might have been acceptable to Jewish sensibility if these ancestral and sworn enemies had somehow become subordinated to Israel, becoming hewers of wood and drawers of water (see Deut. 20:11; Joshua 9:23). But such servitude is clearly not what Isaiah proclaims. These nations were not to be subject to Israel. They were to be made equal with Israel. More shockingly, Israel does not even have the preeminence among them. Rather, Israel is a "third," coming after Egypt and Assyria. God had always spoken of His beloved Israel with such terms of covenant loyalty as "Israel My people," "Israel the work of My hands" (compare Ex. 7:4; Is. 29:23). Now the text applies these terms of endearment to Egypt and Assyria.

In this oracle Isaiah promises that God's love would one day flow so abundantly as to utterly sweep away every single historical distinction—even distinctions God Himself had made and drilled into Israel through His Law and through bitter historical experience. Such promises eclipse anything national Israel experienced (such as the existence of a Jewish temple for the Jewish expatriate workers in Elephantine during the Greek age). Looking at these verses, we see in them our own experience of Jesus, and the salvation in which national distinctions are utterly transcended, so that in Him "there is neither Greek nor Jew, circumcised nor uncircumcised, barbarian, Scythian, slave *nor* free, but Christ *is* all and in all" (Col. 3:11). In this salvation, the nation of Israel indeed possesses no preeminence or privilege. All who come to Christ in humble and repentant faith are accepted on equal terms. The shocking leveling of Israel and their new place among the nations now blessed by God has come to pass before our very eyes.

The Feast of Immortality: Isaiah 25:6–9

The prophets contain many promises of God's help and the blessing that would come from His abiding presence, but perhaps few of these promises go as far as this promise of feasting on Mount Zion.

> And in this mountain
> The LORD of hosts will make for all people
> A feast of choice pieces,
> A feast of wines on the lees. . . .
> And He will destroy on this mountain
> The surface of the covering cast over all people,
> And the veil that is spread over all nations.
> He will swallow up death forever,
> And the Lord GOD will wipe away tears from all faces;
> The rebuke of His people
> He will take away from all the earth . . .
> And it will be said in that day:
> "Behold, this *is* our God;
> We have waited for Him, and He will save us. . . .
> We will be glad and rejoice in His salvation." (Is. 25:6–9)

The promises are indeed staggering. God proclaims that Zion will be the site of a feast of great abundance, the best of the meat, the best of the wine. Moreover, at that feast on Mount Zion He will destroy death, the darkness that covers all people of the earth, the veil of mourning which all nations must wear. He will swallow up death forever, so that all tearstained faces will look to Him with joy. His people will suffer reproach and insult no more, for their God has acted to save the world. A new day of gladness and rejoicing will come at last.

Such staggering promises strain credibility, and certainly can find no fulfillment in the political history of Israel. But we have seen their spiritual fulfillment in Jesus and the salvation that He has brought and offers in the Eucharist, His feast of immortality. On the night in which Jesus was betrayed, He sat with His disciples in an upper room in Mount Zion and made feast for all peoples. The Eucharist He instituted there was indeed "a feast of choice pieces, / A feast of wines on the lees"—that is, a feast of spiritual abundance. For it is through that feast that we experience immortality and eternal life. By His death and resurrection Christ destroyed death, taking away forever that veil spread over all the nations. At this feast we make *anamnesis*, a memorial of that death and resurrection, and participate in its saving power. At this feast we exult over Christ sacramentally present in our midst: "Behold, this *is* our God; / We have waited for Him, and He will save us. . . . / We will be glad and rejoice in His salvation." Given our continual eucharistic experience of these realities, it is not surprising that we have come to see in Isaiah's feast of immortality a prophecy of our own festal assemblies.

Healing for the Blind, Deaf, and Lame: Isaiah 35

The prophecies of Isaiah 35 look forward to a postexilic time of restoration. God would restore the land as He brought His people home, so that they "come to Zion with singing." They would "obtain joy and gladness, / And sorrow and sighing shall flee away" (Is. 35:10). The land, once desolate while they were in exile, would now return to new life.

> The wilderness and the wasteland shall be glad for them,
> And the desert shall rejoice and blossom as the rose;
> It shall blossom abundantly and rejoice,
> Even with joy and singing. . . .

> They shall see the glory of the LORD,
> The excellency of our God.
> . . .
> Then the eyes of the blind shall be opened,
> And the ears of the deaf shall be unstopped.
> Then the lame shall leap like a deer,
> And the tongue of the dumb sing.
> For waters shall burst forth in the wilderness,
> And streams in the desert. (Is. 35:1–6)

Isaiah paints a picture of national rejuvenation and the restoration of vitality and hope.

The prophecy finds partial fulfillment in the return of the exiles from the lands of their captivity, documented and celebrated in the Books of Ezra and Nehemiah, and supported by the postexilic prophets Haggai, Zechariah, and Malachi. A few hardy exiles, longing for home and eager for adventure, braved the hardships of return and struggled valiantly to rebuild a national life long shattered. Those early postexilic days had their share of joy and triumph (Ezra relates how they shouted for joy and praised the Lord when the foundation of the new Temple was laid; Ezra 3:10–13). But there were disappointments as well (Ezra also relates how the older men among them wept while the Temple's foundation was laid). The city walls were built by men carrying swords and spears, so great was the opposition (Neh. 4). In the days of the Maccabees, there was still persecution to be endured, and Israel lost what political sovereignty it had gained under the Persians when the Romans came to occupy their land in the first century BC. Clearly, sorrow and sighing had not yet fled away.

The complete fulfillment of this oracle therefore lies not in any political arrangement or physical rejuvenation of the land, neither before the loss of the Temple in AD 70 nor after the founding of a Jewish state in 1948. It is only through Jesus that sorrow finally flees away. We Christians look at the presence of Jesus of Nazareth in the land and say that in Him we see "the glory of the LORD, / The excellency of our God." In His presence, spiritual aridity gave place to new life, and the desert blossomed. Through His ministry, the eyes of the blind were opened, and the ears of the deaf unstopped; through His miracles the lame man leaped like a deer, and the tongue of the dumb sang.

Christ Himself proclaimed that He was the fulfillment of this ancient oracle. When the disciples of the imprisoned John the Baptizer came to Jesus to demand on John's behalf proof of Jesus' messiahship, the Lord answered them, "Go and tell John the things which you hear and see: *The* blind see and *the* lame walk; *the* lepers are cleansed and *the* deaf hear; *the* dead are raised up and *the* poor have the gospel preached to them" (Matt. 11:2–5). In speaking of the blind seeing, the lame walking, and the deaf hearing, Jesus was citing this oracle. The proof that He was the long-expected Christ was in these miracles of healing and the bestowal of new hope for the poor.

The Servant Songs: Isaiah 40—53

The Servant Songs are a series of oracles declaring the sovereignty of God in the face of Israel's defeat and exile. Some thought this defeat proved that Israel's God was less powerful than the gods of the nations that defeated Israel. These oracles proclaim the contrary—that Israel's catastrophic defeat was the will of Yahweh. Yahweh, who willed to send Israel into exile for rebellion against Him, was now restoring Israel to the land by the exercise of that same sovereign will. Since Yahweh was the one true Lord over all the nations, whose power compared to His was like a drop from a bucket, like dust on the scales, all things were His servants. Israel was His servant (Is. 44:1f), the Persian king Cyrus was His servant (Is. 45:1f), and the king of Israel was His servant (Is. 42:1f; 49:1f; 52:13f). In the commentary that follows, we will focus on the oracles that concern the king of Israel, the messianic Servant of Yahweh. All of these Servant Songs about Israel's king emphasize the king's humility, to show more clearly that the sovereign power belongs to God.

In the **first Servant Song**, we read the following:

"Behold! My Servant whom I uphold,
My Elect One *in whom* My soul delights!

> I have put My Spirit upon Him;
> He will bring forth justice to the Gentiles.
> He will not cry out, nor raise *His voice,*
> Nor cause His voice to be heard in the street.
> A bruised reed He will not break,
> And smoking flax He will not quench; . . .
> He will not fail nor be discouraged,
> Till He has established justice in the earth;
> And the coastlands shall wait for His law." (Is. 42:1–4)

This oracle portrays the king as humble and peaceful. Unlike the blustering and boasting kings who loudly declared their might and their power to conquer (compare the boasts of the Assyrian king in Is. 36:4–20), God's servant makes no such boasts, no such self-promotion. On the contrary, he does not cry out or raise his voice in pride. He is gentle and takes care not to break the bruised reed or quench the dimly burning wick. Yet despite his refusal of armed military hubris, he will bring forth justice to all the nations, for God's Spirit rests upon him. He will continue in his path of humility, trusting in his God, until he has established justice in the earth. God will vindicate him and make him victorious, so that even the distant coastlands will wait expectantly for his instruction (Heb. *torah*) and will follow his will.

It is in Jesus that this oracle of peace is fulfilled. He is the One upon whom the Spirit of God rested so palpably. He is the One whose law went forth in the world, so that even distant coastlands ring with the Christian praises of God and strive to fulfill His law. But more than this, unlike other leaders who promoted their own cause with vigor, Jesus refused such self-promotion. He healed the many who flocked about Him, and could have instructed them to publicize their healings and tell everyone about the glorious healer. But He did not. Rather, He "warned them not to make Him known" (Matt. 12:16). Christ refused to use His many miracles as a form of advertising. When He cleansed a leper, He warned him not to tell anyone of how he was healed (Matt. 8:4). When He opened the eyes of two blind men, He warned them also to tell no one (Matt. 9:30). When He raised a young girl from death, He gave order to her parents that no one should know of this (Mark 5:43). Such refusal to let others know of one's great deeds is rare in men, and more rare still in kings and those seeking followers. But it fulfills the ancient words about this gentle king, who relied solely upon God for his success.

In the **second Servant Song**, we read:

"Listen, O coastlands, to Me,
And take heed, you peoples from afar!
The Lord has called Me from the womb;
From the matrix of My mother He has made mention of
    My name.
And He has made My mouth like a sharp sword;
In the shadow of His hand He has hidden Me,
And made Me a polished shaft;
In His quiver He has hidden Me.

"And He said to me,
'You *are* My servant, O Israel,
In whom I will be glorified.'
Then I said, 'I have labored in vain,
I have spent my strength for nothing and in vain;
Yet surely my just reward *is* with the Lord,
And my work with my God.'

"And now the Lord says,
Who formed Me from the womb *to be* His Servant,
To bring Jacob back to Him,
So that Israel is gathered to Him. . . .
Indeed He says,
'It is too small a thing that You should be My Servant
To raise up the tribes of Jacob,
And to restore the preserved ones of Israel;
I will also give You as a light to the Gentiles,
That You should be My salvation to the ends of the earth.'"

Thus says the Lord,
The Redeemer of Israel, their Holy One,

> To Him whom man despises,
> To Him whom the nation abhors,
> To the Servant of rulers:
> "Kings shall see and arise,
> Princes also shall worship,
> Because of the LORD who is faithful,
> The Holy One of Israel;
> And He has chosen You." (Is. 49:1–7)

Once again the prophet emphasizes the humility of God's royal servant. The king is powerful in God's hands, like a sharp arrow in the hand of a skillful bowman. But that arrow is hidden in God's quiver, like a secret weapon, its true worth unknown to others. God may have declared to the king that he embodied all His purposes for Israel, but as far as the king himself was concerned, he had toiled in vain, for none knew of his glory. But his reward remained with God, and He would remedy this. Not only would the king be honored by Israel as he restored its tribes to God, he would be honored by the faraway nations also. Though the king was now despised and abhorred by his own nation and was treated like a servant by its rulers, God would see to it that kings would see his glory and arise before him; their princes would bow down in obeisance because God had chosen him.

This Servant Song is even more astonishing than its predecessor, for it portrays the king as suffering terrible humiliation. What king of Israel was ever despised and abhorred by his own people? What king ever went from such rags of dishonor to the riches of international recognition and preeminence? No political king ever played such a part, but we see how Jesus fulfills this role with exactitude. He is the One whose true glory went unrecognized by the rulers of this age, so that they rejected Him as worthless, even though He was the Lord of glory (1 Cor. 2:8). He was despised by His own people, abhorred by them even though He was their true King, and betrayed to a Roman cross. And it was through Him that not only were the faithful in Israel gathered into one, but the nations also were drawn to His light (John 11:52; Acts 13:47). He alone can lay claim to being the messianic Servant of Yahweh.

In the **third Servant Song**, we read these words:

"The Lord G<small>OD</small> has given Me
The tongue of the learned,
That I should know how to speak
A word in season to *him who is* weary.
. . .
The Lord G<small>OD</small> has opened My ear;
And I was not rebellious,
Nor did I turn away.
I gave My back to those who struck *Me,*
And My cheeks to those who plucked out the beard;
I did not hide My face from shame and spitting.

"For the Lord G<small>OD</small> will help Me;
Therefore I will not be disgraced;
Therefore I have set My face like a flint,
And I know that I will not be ashamed.
He is near who justifies Me;
Who will contend with Me?
Let us stand together.
Who *is* My adversary?
Let him come near Me.
Surely the Lord G<small>OD</small> will help Me;
Who *is* he *who* will condemn Me?
Indeed they will all grow old like a garment;
The moth will eat them up." (Is. 50:4–9)

In this Song we see an escalation of opposition to the Servant. In the second Song, the prophet spoke of the Servant as one despised and abhorred. Here we read of him being smitten, his beard plucked out, his face being spit upon. Such brutality is shocking enough in itself. It is even more horrifying when a king is thus humiliated. Yet the king accepted it all with serenity, maintaining his posture as a disciple of God, a humble student before his teacher. He did not endure these atrocities while squirming and resisting. Rather, he gave his back freely to those who struck him, and his cheeks to those who would tear out his beard. He did not even try to resist when his foes spit into his face—a terrible insult in an honor-shame culture such as that of the Near East.

He allowed himself to be disgraced in this way because he was confident that God would thoroughly vindicate him. These outrages were not to be the last word. His foes would at length see God vindicate him.

As we read these words, we are confronted immediately with the Passion of our own Lord. Jesus was the humble teacher, One given wisdom from God so that His mere word could sustain the weary. Though He knew that humiliation and death awaited Him in Jerusalem, He also "steadfastly set His face" to go there (Luke 9:51). Once there, He was arrested, struck, spit upon in the face (Matt. 26:67). Yet He endured all this with serenity, knowing God would raise Him from the dead on the third day. This Servant Song sang the story of the death of Jesus. We do not have to read anything arbitrarily into the text. The text itself shouts to us what we have seen with our own eyes.

The **fourth Servant Song** is perhaps the most familiar of all. It reads:

Behold, My Servant shall deal prudently;
He shall be exalted and extolled and be very high.
Just as many were astonished at you,
So His visage was marred more than any man,
And His form more than the sons of men;
So shall He sprinkle [or *startle*] many nations.
. . . .
For He shall grow up before Him as a tender plant,
And as a root out of dry ground.
He has no form or comeliness;
And when we see Him,
There is no beauty that we should desire Him.
He is despised and rejected by men,
A Man of sorrows and acquainted with grief.
And we hid, as it were, *our* faces from Him;
He was despised, and we did not esteem Him.

Surely He has borne our griefs
And carried our sorrows;
Yet we esteemed Him stricken,

Smitten by God, and afflicted.
But He *was* wounded for our transgressions,
He was bruised for our iniquities;
The chastisement for our peace *was* upon Him,
And by His stripes we are healed.
All we like sheep have gone astray;
We have turned, every one, to his own way;
And the LORD has laid on Him the iniquity of us all.

He was oppressed and He was afflicted,
Yet He opened not His mouth;
He was led as a lamb to the slaughter,
And as a sheep before its shearers is silent,
So He opened not His mouth.
He was taken from prison and from judgment,
And who will declare His generation?
For He was cut off from the land of the living;
For the transgressions of My people He was stricken.
And they made His grave with the wicked—
But with the rich at His death,
Because He had done no violence,
Nor *was any* deceit in His mouth.

Yet it pleased the LORD to bruise Him;
He has put *Him* to grief.
When You make His soul an offering for sin,
He shall see *His* seed, He shall prolong *His* days . . .
He shall see the labor of His soul, *and* be satisfied.
By His knowledge My righteous Servant shall justify many,
For He shall bear their iniquities.
Therefore I will divide Him a portion with the great . . .
Because He poured out His soul unto death,
And He was numbered with the transgressors,
And He bore the sin of many,
And made intercession for the transgressors.
   (Is. 52:13—53:12)

In this passage the humiliation of the king described in the earlier Servant Songs reaches its horrifying climax. Just as Israel astonished the world by the devastation it suffered though its military defeats, so the king by his suffering will astonish many nations, who will be startled to see how marred he has become. The king had no regal dignity that any should take serious notice of him. Everyone despised and rejected him, as they would write off a sick and dying man, a man cursed by God. He was pierced, he was scourged, he suffered a travesty of justice. Like a helpless lamb led to slaughter, he meekly accepted all this affliction and even death, not uttering a single protest. After his death, he was buried with criminals as the final indignity.

Yet all his sufferings were given by God, that by them his people might be saved. It was through his piercing that his people's transgressions were forgiven; it was through his chastisement and flogging that his people had peace, through his scourging that they were healed. All the bruising and crushing affliction he endured came from God, that through him the multitude of God's people might be justified and have their iniquities carried away. Because the innocent Servant bore this injustice and sacrificed himself as a sin offering, God would vindicate him. His grave would be with rich and honorable men; he would live again, prolong his days, and see his offspring. He would receive the honor due to great men and be satisfied.

The difficulty in finding anything remotely like this in the history of Israel's kings or imagining that a king could suffer such things has long led others to question who this Servant could be. As the Ethiopian eunuch once asked of Philip, "I ask you, of whom does the prophet say this, of himself or of some other man?" (Acts 8:34). Those knowing only worldly kings find this passage an impenetrable mystery. But we Christians know of whom the prophet speaks. Looking at this passage, we are plunged into the final days of the Lord's life. It is as if we are reading the Gospel record and not an ancient oracle.

Jesus was the One whose countenance, marred more than any man's through scourging and crucifixion, startled the nations. He was the One who was despised and rejected, and from whom the people of Israel hid their faces and asked for Barabbas instead. He was the One led as a sheep to the slaughter, who opened not His mouth to defend

Himself, so that Pilate wondered greatly. He was the One whose life was taken away in a travesty of justice, through oppression and judgment. He was the One numbered with transgressors and executed as a criminal between two thieves. He was the One who poured out His soul to death, justifying many, carrying away the sins of the world. He was the One who should have been thrown into a felon's grave, yet was buried honorably in the tomb of the rich Joseph of Arimathea. He was the One who rose from the dead, prolonging His days and ever living to make intercession for us sinners.

These final notes of the long Servant Songs form the eternal song of praise of the Church of God.

Kingship: Expectation and Fulfillment

The messianic prophecies of Isaiah declare the glories of the coming king, and all expected this king to be a king like all the other kings. That is, the people expected a king who would sit on a throne, surrounded by courtiers, supported by an army and by all the political apparatus of the state. He would be wiser and more righteous than all the previous kings, of course, and his reign would usher in a time of unprecedented prosperity and worldwide peace. But he would reign from a royal palace, commanding all the pomp, power, and privilege that have always attended those in such estate. Thus he would be instantly identifiable by all the people as their lawful political ruler. Those reading Isaiah's words expected kingship to be the political reality they had always known (though the extinction of that reality at the Exile, with all the trauma reflected in Ps. 89:38f, offered a faint hint that God's faithfulness did not hinge on political realities).

No one in those days could have foreseen how those messianic prophecies would actually be fulfilled. They expected the Anointed One to be a king, not a carpenter, and to wield all the political power usually wielded by kings, not to be a powerless field preacher with no place to lay His head. They thought the Messiah might have to endure a military defeat or two on the way to final triumph and world domination, but they never thought He would die on a cross, abandoned by all. By fulfilling the messianic prophecies in Jesus of Nazareth, God overturned all the expectations of man.

This was part of God's eternal plan, the mystery "which in other ages was not made known to the sons of men," the mystery "which from the beginning of the ages has been hidden in God" (Eph. 3:5, 9). The political Messiah Israel expected would have been subject to all the difficulties and moral compromises that attend any political regime. It would have required national borders, armies to guard those borders, bloody wars to defend attacks on those borders. It would have required taxation, foreign policy, immigration restrictions, secret service operatives. It would have divided the world into "us" and "them." And like all merely earthly empires that rose, it would eventually fall, so that future historians would write a book entitled, *The Rise and Fall of the Messianic Empire.*

This was not God's plan. God planned to transcend the timeless and deadly dichotomy of "us" and "them," to tear down the dividing wall that separated Jew and Gentile. He planned to "gather together in one the children of God who were scattered abroad" (John 11:52), to create a new people who shared a new nature. He planned a Kingdom which had no borders, needed no armies, and would need to fight no bloody wars to defend its sovereignty. This Kingdom would have no oppressive taxation, for its King was supported by the power of God alone, not by any human resources. It would have no foreign policy, no immigration restrictions, for all foreigners could instantly become citizens of this Kingdom through faith and baptism, without change of place or earthly nationality. In Christ, God was transforming the very nature of kingship and power, of salvation and defeat, of peace and war. Everything was redefined and transfigured. In Him, "old things have passed away; behold, all things have become new" (2 Cor. 5:17). In this Kingdom, God made all things new (see Rev. 21:5), for it was only through this transformation that His salvation could extend to all the world, and all men could find their way home.

This disjunction of expectation and fulfillment remained hidden from the eyes of men until God brought it to fulfillment in Christ. By doing so, He used the free choices of men, their loyalty as well as their betrayal, to carry out His will. As St. Paul said, the people, "because they did not know Him, nor even the voices of the Prophets which are read every Sabbath, have fulfilled *them* in condemning *Him*" (Acts 13:27). The difficulty men had in discerning the true nature of messianic kingship was the very thing God used to fulfill His plan. Thus God made fools of the earth's wise men and proved that His foolishness was wiser than men, and His weakness, stronger than men (1 Cor. 1:25). None of the wise in Isaiah's day or after foresaw this. And (to quote a non-biblical author), "Who of all the wise could have foreseen it? Or, if they are wise, why should they expect to know it, until the hour had struck?"[7] In Christ, God brought the unexpected to pass, fulfilling the dreams of men beyond what they could have dared to hope.

The New Covenant: Jeremiah 31

The covenant with Israel God made through Moses was ending in disaster, wrath, and exile. Israel had continued to rebel against God and refuse the persistent call of the prophets. The divine patience had at last come to an end, and the long prophesied judgment was falling. Jeremiah lived and prophesied in those terrible and terrifying days, and had himself warned Israel over and over again that judgment was coming.

But he also offered words of hope, encouragement, and restoration. One of these words concerned the new covenant God would make with them:

> "Behold, the days are coming, says the LORD, when I will make a new covenant with the house of Israel and with the house of Judah—not according to the covenant that I made with their fathers in the day *that* I took them by the hand to lead them out of the land of Egypt, My covenant which they broke, though I was a husband to them, says the LORD. But this *is* the covenant that I will make with the house of Israel after those days, says the LORD: I will put My law in their minds, and write it on their hearts; and I will be their God, and they shall be My people. No more shall every man teach his neighbor, and every man his

---

[7] J.R.R. Tolkien, *Lord of the Rings*, Book II, Chapter 3, "The Council of Elrond."

brother, saying, 'Know the LORD,' for they all shall know Me, from the least of them to the greatest of them, says the LORD. For I will forgive their iniquity, and their sin I will remember no more." (Jer. 31:31–34)

The old covenant had foundered on the people's rebellion and had brought only death and destruction. But better days were coming, when God would make a new covenant with His people. In this covenant, the Law would not remain an external decree, written on stone and guarded by priests. God would make His Law an internal force, written on their hearts. There would be no further necessity for the prophets to rebuke apostasy and threaten judgment, for all the people would know God and serve Him in truth. God would forgive their acts of apostasy, which had led them into exile, and remember those sins no more.

It is easy to miss the revolutionary nature of these words. The prophets had always urged the people to return to the old ways (compare Jer. 6:16 as typical: "Ask for the old paths, where the good way *is*, and walk in it"). But here the old ways are utterly discarded as inadequate. The salvation God will work among them will make the old covenant unnecessary. This prophecy is similar to the revolutionary one found in Jeremiah 3:16: "'Then it shall come to pass, when you are multiplied and increased in the land in those days,' says the LORD, 'that they will say no more, "The ark of the covenant of the LORD." It shall not come to mind, nor shall they remember it, nor shall they visit *it*, nor shall it be made anymore.'" Given that the Ark was absolutely central and foundational to Israel's worship of God, this prophecy looks to nothing less than a complete reordering of their religious life.

We believers recognize such a complete reordering through Jesus Christ. The Ark, lost in the exile and never recovered, has become irrelevant through the access to God He provides, along with the Temple, its priesthood, and its sacrifices. Through the Spirit of Christ, the Law is written in the human heart, so that its power can overcome the internal grip of sin and death (Rom. 8:1–4). The forgiveness that flows from His Cross makes the sacrifices of the Temple unnecessary and the Old Covenant that mandated them obsolete.

This is the hidden significance of Jeremiah's prophecy. When God said, "Their sins and their lawless deeds I will remember no more," this implied the elimination of any need for further sacrifices, for "where there is remission of these, *there is* no longer an offering for sin" (Heb. 10:17–18). The new covenant foreseen by Jeremiah involves the complete transcendence of all the old ways of Moses' Law.

The Outpouring of the Spirit: Joel 2, Isaiah 44, Ezekiel 36

In the days of the Old Testament, the Spirit was given only to select individuals, such as kings, prophets, and judges. But Joel and other prophets looked to the day when God would pour out His Spirit upon all His people, down to the most humble. As Joel predicted:

> "And it shall come to pass afterward
> That I will pour out My Spirit on all flesh;
> Your sons and your daughters shall prophesy,
> Your old men shall dream dreams,
> Your young men shall see visions.
> And also on *My* menservants and on *My* maidservants
> I will pour out My Spirit in those days.

> "And I will show wonders in the heavens and in the earth:
> Blood and fire and pillars of smoke.
> The sun shall be turned into darkness,
> And the moon into blood,
> Before the coming of the great and awesome day of the LORD.
> And it shall come to pass
> *That* whoever calls on the name of the LORD
> Shall be saved." (Joel 2:28–32)

Joel was not alone in anticipating the bestowal of the Spirit to all God's people. One of Isaiah's Servant Songs promises, "For I will pour water on him who is thirsty, / And floods on the dry ground; / I will pour My Spirit on your descendants, / And My blessing on your offspring" (Is. 44:3). The prophet Ezekiel also looked to the day when all Israel would be full of the Spirit and would obey the Lord: "Then I will sprinkle clean water on you, and you shall be clean; I will cleanse you from all your filthiness and from all your idols. I will give you a new heart and put a new spirit within you; I will take the heart of stone out of your flesh and give you a heart of flesh. I will put My Spirit within you and cause you to walk in My statutes, and you will keep My judgments and do *them*" (Ezek. 36:25-27). In these latter days, the outpouring of the Spirit gave assurance that the people would serve the Lord in holiness, and that His blessing would remain on their land.

The Day of Pentecost, coming with celestial fireworks, announced to all that the last days had come, and that God was indeed pouring out His Spirit upon all flesh. Now it was not simply prophets, kings, and sages who had access to divine wisdom and intimate knowledge of God's will. All Israel's sons and daughters had such access, even the lowliest male and female slaves. Now even fishermen, such as our Lord's first disciples, could become most wise in the knowledge of God. On the Day of Pentecost, the prophetic Spirit was shed abroad upon all, as their supernatural tongues of prophecy showed. Little over a month before the Day of Pentecost, those present in Jerusalem saw the sun turned to darkness at midday when Jesus hung on the cross (Luke 23:44-45). Clearly, the ancient words were coming true before their eyes.

Now, in conformity with this prophecy, everyone who in faith calls on the Name of the Lord can be saved. As Peter announced to the breathless crowd, if they would repent and be baptized in the Name of Jesus Christ, they too would receive the gift of the Holy Spirit (Acts 2:38). Thousands did. We believers ever since have experienced in our baptism and chrismation the promise of the prophets, when God cleansed us of our sins with clean water, gave us a heart of flesh for our former heart of stone, and put His Spirit within us. The prophetic anticipation of a universal outpouring of the Spirit is fulfilled in the sacramental mysteries of the Church.

The Word from Zion: Micah 4

Many of the prophets anticipated a renewal of Jerusalem, so that it became the source for God's saving presence in all the world. Jerusalem, once a faithful city full of justice, had become a prostitute, a den of murderers (Is. 1:21). All the prophets longed for her cleansing and restoration. Micah was only one of a great number of those who wanted the daughter of Zion to turn to God and fulfill her glorious destiny. In the coming days, she would.

Concerning this, Micah wrote:

> Now it shall come to pass in the latter days
> *That* the mountain of the Lord's house
> Shall be established on the top of the mountains,
> And shall be exalted above the hills;
> And peoples shall flow to it.
> Many nations shall come and say,
> "Come, and let us go up to the mountain of the Lord,
> To the house of the God of Jacob;
> He will teach us His ways,
> And we shall walk in His paths."
> For out of Zion the law shall go forth,
> And the word of the Lord from Jerusalem.
> He shall judge between many peoples,
> And rebuke strong nations afar off;
> They shall beat their swords into plowshares,
> And their spears into pruning hooks;
> Nation shall not lift up sword against nation,
> Neither shall they learn war anymore.
>
> But everyone shall sit under his vine and under his fig tree,
> And no one shall make *them* afraid;
> For the mouth of the Lord of hosts has spoken. (Micah 4:1–4)

This prophecy envisions a restored Jerusalem, blessed by God and ruled over by its wise and mighty king. Under this messianic king, the whole world would come to see the glory of Israel's God, as Israel assumed a place of prominence among the nations. That is what the oracle means by saying that Mount Zion would be established as the highest of the mountains, higher than all the other hills/nations. Pilgrims from these nations would come to Zion to seek the wisdom of its king and the favor of its God. The word of the king would be sent to all those nations, and his law and instruction (Heb. *torah*) would govern the peoples so that they would walk in peace. As the Gentile nations allowed themselves to be guided by Zion's king, wars would cease and weapons would be turned to other uses. Every man would enjoy prosperity, sitting under his own vine and fig tree in security and happiness. Thus Jerusalem would be the center and source of peace for the world, as the word of its king went forth into all the earth.

This centrality of Jerusalem in the purposes of God is a major theme in the prophets. In Isaiah 60, God bids Jerusalem, "Arise, shine; / For your light has come!" and goes on to describe her future glory when nations would come from every direction to offer their gifts, worship at the Temple, and adorn the Lord's house. In Isaiah 62, God promises that Jerusalem's righteousness will "[go] forth as brightness, / And her salvation as a lamp *that* burns." She will be called by all, "Sought Out, A City Not Forsaken" (Is. 62:12).

So great will be the change in Zion's fortunes that Isaiah speaks of God creating "new heavens and a new earth . . . I create Jerusalem *as* a rejoicing" (Is. 65:17–18). In Zephaniah's prophecies we read:

> Sing, O daughter of Zion!
> Shout, O Israel!
> Be glad and rejoice with all *your* heart,
> O daughter of Jerusalem!
> The LORD has taken away your judgments,
> He has cast out your enemy.
> The King of Israel, the LORD, *is* in your midst;
> You shall see disaster no more. (Zeph. 3:14–15)

In Haggai God promises that He "will shake all nations, and they shall come to the Desire of All Nations, and I will fill this temple with glory" (Hag. 2:7).

Zechariah has many words of comfort for Zion, not least of which is the promise that all nations will come as pilgrims to keep her feasts: "And it shall come to pass *that* everyone who is left of all the nations which came against Jerusalem shall go up from year to year to worship the King, the LORD of hosts, and to keep the Feast of Tabernacles" (Zech. 14:16). Ever since God made a covenant with David and promised to bless him and his descendants, Jerusalem has been the city of prophecy, destined for glory. As the Psalmist said, "For the LORD has chosen Zion; / He has desired *it* for His dwelling place: / 'This *is* My resting place forever; / Here I will dwell, for I have desired it'" (Ps. 132:13–14).

How were these prophecies fulfilled? Even as kingship in Israel was transfigured so that the king was no longer a political figure but a transcendent one, so with the destiny of Zion. One reading these prophecies might expect a political fulfillment, with a king reigning in Zion and his political decrees, treaties, and policies issuing forth from the capital through the normal diplomatic channels. But just as the messianic Kingdom was spiritual, so was the destiny of Jerusalem. The king's word did not go forth in diplomatic pouches, but through the lips of apostles. His word did not consist of political treaties and alliances, but of the saving Gospel of the grace of God.

After our Lord's resurrection, He revealed to His apostles how the Scriptures were fulfilled in Him. He said they predicted not only His own sufferings and resurrection, but also that "repentance and remission of sins should be preached in His name to all nations, beginning at Jerusalem" (Luke 24:45–47). Note that Jerusalem's role as the source of the saving universal proclamation is said to be "written" in the Scriptures.

These Jerusalem prophecies find their fulfillment in the Gospel. Christ's presence in the Holy City, cleansing its Temple during the last week of His sojourn there, and His abiding spiritual presence in the Church in Jerusalem transformed the city, so that one could indeed confess that the king of Israel was in its midst (Zeph. 3:14). Zion could arise and shine, for its light had come (Is. 60:1). It had been now recreated for rejoicing, as God in Christ made all things new (Is. 65:17–18). The apostles, sent out from Jerusalem into all the earth (Acts 1:8), carried a word of peace capable of restoring all the nations.

The spiritual nature of Jerusalem's destiny mirrors the spiritual nature of the Kingdom of God in this age. Jews in our Lord's time expected the coming Kingdom to be political, military, visible to all. They expected it to come like a eucatastrophe, an explosion of goodness,

The Prophets

overturning the political order of the world. In the worldly kingdom they expected, evil men would be forcibly eliminated and a new order immediately (and violently) established.

The Lord's many parables teach otherwise. The Kingdom leaves the outer order of the world intact (for now), so that evil and good men continue to thrive side by side, like tares growing among wheat (Matt. 13:24–31). The Kingdom bears fruit only in the lives of those able to receive it, even as seed bears fruit only when cast into good and fertile ground (Matt. 13:3–8). It works slowly and invisibly within the hearts of men, even as leaven works within a batch of flour (Matt. 13:33). In short, the Kingdom of God is present in the world during this age as a spiritual force, a sacramental power. It is only at the end of the age that it will overturn the established order and find its consummation in the age to come.

In the present age, therefore, the earthly Jerusalem in Palestine had a spiritual role to play, not a political one. It fulfilled that role as the home of the Mother Church, the center from which the Gospel was sent out to many peoples and strong nations, that they might learn the ways of God and beat their swords into plowshares for the sake of Christ.

CHAPTER 5

THE WRITINGS: SINGING THE LORD'S SONG

The Third Division of the Hebrew Bible

THE HEBREW BIBLE HAS THREE PARTS: (1) the Law, consisting of the first five books of Moses; (2) the Prophets, consisting of the historical books (the so-called "Former Prophets") and the Prophets (the so-called Latter Prophets); and (3) the Writings, consisting of the "Books of Truth" (Psalms, Proverbs, Job), the "Five Scrolls" (Song of Songs, Ruth, Lamentations, Ecclesiastes, Esther), and the rest of the "Writings" (Daniel, Ezra-Nehemiah, Chronicles). Since this volume offers a Christian approach to the Hebrew Scriptures, for convenience we adopt this Hebrew classification of the scriptural books. All classifications are somewhat arbitrary, of course, for it was not until later, when all the books could be bound within a single volume, that such classifications could arise in the first place.

To these books of the classic Jewish canon, we Christians who value the Fathers also add the other books of the so-called "Apocrypha" or Deuterocanonicals, such as the Books of Sirach, Wisdom, Maccabees, Tobit, Judith, and Esdras. (The Orthodox term for these books is *Anaginoskomena*, the "Readable" Books, which may be read liturgically in church.)

Our Lord's words about the Scriptures reflect this threefold classification, for He referred to the Scriptures as "the Law of Moses and the Prophets and the Psalms" (Luke 24:44; this latter perhaps standing for all the rest of "the Writings" as well). The threefold classification is also reflected in the words of the Prologue to Sirach, where the translator speaks of "the Law and the Prophets and the others that followed them" and of "the Law and the Prophets and other books of our fathers." By using this classification of the biblical books, I make no statement about their dating. (The Book of Lamentations, for example, though a part of the Writings and not the Prophets, was classically thought to date from Jeremiah's time, with Jeremiah as its author.) We begin by looking at the Psalms.

The Psalms: Celebrating the Power of the King

The Psalter is a collection of songs, written by a variety of authors, and gathered into a series of five collections in one book. King David, lauded as the "sweet psalmist of Israel" in 2 Samuel 23:1, is the traditional author of many of the psalms throughout the collection. Some of these psalms exult in the royal power and glorious destiny of the House of David, reigning from Zion, his city. Such are Psalms 2, 45, and 72.

Psalm 2 portrays a hostile international alliance conspiring against the House of David, reigning over the world from Zion. In this psalm, all "the nations rage." Refusing submission to the House of David in Zion, "The kings of the earth set themselves, / And the rulers take counsel together, / Against the LORD and against His Anointed" King [Gr., His *Christos*]. They are determined to "break Their bonds in pieces" and refuse submission to God's beneficent rule and treaties. The Lord "who sits in the heavens shall laugh" in scorn at such folly, saying, "Yet I have set My King / On My holy hill of Zion." The rebellious nations can do whatever they want. Resistance is futile. Zion's king confesses, "I will declare the decree: / The LORD has said to Me, / 'You *are* My Son, / Today I have begotten You. / Ask of Me, and I will give *You* / The nations *for* Your inheritance.'" Thus the rule of Zion's king is assured, and the kings should "be wise" and submit to it.

This psalm is extremely triumphal. It portrays the king of Israel, sitting on the throne of David, as God's adopted son. (The day of adoption was the day the king was made king, becoming Yahweh's adopted son, "begotten" by Him, and thus under His protection and care.) All the nations were his by right, given by Yahweh. The nations could attempt rebellion if they wished, but at the end of the day they must "serve the LORD with fear" and submit to His son, the adopted king of Israel. Otherwise the Lord would "be angry, / And you perish *in* the way."

Here we can hardly fail to see Jesus, the anointed king, as the fulfillment of this poetry (see Acts 4:23–28). The all-powerful alliance portrayed in this psalm as united against God's *Christos* is fulfilled in the alliance of the powerful Jewish ruler Herod and the powerful Roman ruler Pontius Pilate, united against Jesus to destroy Him (compare Luke 23:6–12). Herod and Pilate were the unwitting representatives of the prophesied alliance of Jew and Gentile (i.e. the whole world) against the Lord. Yet their plots were futile, for God willed to vindicate Jesus and establish Him upon His heavenly throne as God's only-begotten Son, even as Yahweh in the psalm installed His king upon Zion.

The ancient poetry found political fulfillment in the final days of Christ's life. The fine poetic details of the ancient prophecy were transposed to the harsh historical realities of contemporary front-page news. The international alliance pictured in the psalm hardened into fulfillment in the backroom deals between a Jewish ruler and a Roman procurator. But whatever the discontinuities between poetry and fulfillment, the spirit of the prophecy was abundantly fulfilled: the powerful of the earth united against the lone and lonely *Christos*, who was destined to rule the nations with the divine rod of iron.

Psalm 45 is a wedding psalm, a song of love praising the royal groom. The psalmist praises the king for his military prowess: "Gird Your sword upon *Your* thigh, O Mighty One, / With Your glory and Your majesty. / And in Your majesty ride prosperously because of truth, humility, *and* righteousness." His harem consists of "kings' daughters," and "at Your right hand stands the queen," his royal bride, "in gold from Ophir." In the midst of this psalm we find the astonishing words: "Your throne, O God, *is* forever and ever." That is, the king is called "God" [Heb. *Elohim*].

Other translations are possible. One marginal rendering suggests one might translate the words as, "God is your throne," though this rendering suffers from the disadvantage of incomprehensibility. How can God be a throne? The RSV does its best, translating the phrase "your divine throne endures for ever and ever," though the difficulty remains, since even in this translation the psalmist identifies the king's earthly throne with God's.

These words portray the psalmist calling the king *Elohim*. It is not the only time the word was used in the Psalms to describe human beings: Psalm 82:1 uses the word *elohim*, "gods," to describe the human judges, since divine authority over life and death is given to them. But Psalm 45 pushes the boundary between deity and humanity even further, since the word *Elohim* used to describe the king is not used in the plural as a common noun to describe men, but rather in the singular as the proper name of God. It is a daring poetic image—and one that invites further Christian reflection.

The Letter to the Hebrews grasps the nettle and boldly applies the words to Christ God (Heb. 1:8–9). In Him, poetry becomes history (or "myth becomes fact," to quote C.S. Lewis[8]). Descriptions of Israel's king that were originally simply metaphor and poetry have become historical reality in the life of Jesus of Nazareth. He is God incarnate, *Elohim* made flesh, and His Father and God "anointed You / With the oil of gladness more than Your companions," the other kings of the earth, exalting Him to His right hand in heaven. This psalmist, celebrating the nuptial glory of the king, points us to Jesus.

Psalm 72 also celebrates the glory of the House of David. The psalm, ascribed to Solomon, prays that the king will be a blessing to his people, "coming down like rain," "like showers *that* water the earth" (in the Middle East, rain was always a blessing). The psalmist foresaw the king's dominion extending "from sea to sea," from the Red Sea to the Mediterranean, and "from the [Euphrates] River to the ends of the earth." In this global extension of the king's influence, even "Those who dwell in the wilderness will bow before Him," and the far-distant "kings of Tarshish" would bring presents as tribute. The "kings of Sheba and Seba" in southern Arabia would "offer gifts," as "all nations" would "serve Him." No historical king of Israel enjoyed such global prominence and

---

[8] In his article by the same title, published in *World Dominion*, vol. XXII, 1944.

power, although Solomon's extensive trading operations gave Israel an economic hegemony never before imagined. The poetry looks past the horizons of history to a messianic glory.

Although the Magi came to offer gifts to the young Christ child, the Lord Jesus did not command such international allegiances during His earthly lifetime. But the psalm still finds fulfillment in Him and His Kingdom as earthly kings from all over the world entered the Church and offered themselves and their wealth in His service. The obeisance of the nations, anticipated by psalmist and prophet alike (see Is. 60:4–14; Micah 7:16–17; Haggai 2:7), was fulfilled in Byzantium, as nations across the Roman world came to serve the Jewish Messiah and "bow before Him." In seeing how the ancient poetry is fulfilled in Christ, we need to look not only to our Lord's brief earthly ministry, but also to His ongoing reign at the right hand of God and His presence in His body, the Church.

In such royal psalms as Psalms 2, 45, and 72 we read of the poetic aspirations of the House of David. These psalms were not meant as records of historical realities, or even predictions of future ones, but rather as celebrations of hoped-for possibilities they felt were offered them by God's promise to David. Their kingdom was a small one in comparison with the superpowers of their day such as Egypt, their national strength was slight, and their culture somewhat primitive. Yet the God in their midst who had entered into covenant with their king was the one true God, beside whom the gods of the other nations were nothing. This meant Israel could trust their future was a glorious one, and their king was destined for great things. These psalms portray that greatness. The psalms speak of the king as one against whom the powerful of the world unite and whom they oppose in vain. They refer to the king as God, enthroned and ruling over men, and portray the king as receiving homage from all the kings of the earth.

We Christians look first to our experience of Jesus, and only then to these glorious psalms, and we see how our experience of the Lord fits perfectly with the ancient poetry. We see how the powerful forces of Herod and Pilate united to oppose Jesus, even as the psalm spoke of world forces united to oppose Zion's king. We see how Jesus called Himself the "I AM" and received the adoration of Thomas, who called Him "Lord and God" (John 8:58; 20:28), even as the old psalm called the king "God." We see how all the nations of the world are bowing before Christ as they enter His Church, even as the psalms spoke of the king receiving the submission of all the world's peoples. Such congruences can only mean that these psalms spoke of the glory of Christ. David, who walked with God, was not just a poet, but a prophetic one, and his words were imbued with a deeper meaning than anyone of his day could have guessed.

The Psalms:
Lamenting the Betrayal of the King

As well as royal psalms celebrating the glory of the King, the Psalter contains a number of psalms lamenting suffering, disaster, and betrayal in the House of David. Such are Psalms 22, 41, 69, and 109.

Psalm 22 opens with a cry of dereliction: "My God, my God, why have You forsaken Me?" The psalmist feels abandoned by God, for he is the "reproach of men, and despised by the people." In his misery, the people mock his pain, saying, "He trusted in the LORD, let Him rescue Him; / Let Him deliver Him, since He delights in Him!" The suffering psalmist is encircled by his foes, who are strong as bulls, hostile as roaring lions eager to devour. He is surrounded by "the congregation of the wicked," who have pierced his hands and feet. They have robbed him of everything, including his very clothes, casting lots for them as a final indignity.

Then, suddenly, all changes. After crying, "Save Me from the lion's mouth / And from the horns of the wild oxen!" (i.e. from imminent and certain death), the psalmist cries, "I will declare Your name to My brethren; / In the midst of the assembly I will praise You." Not only has God delivered him, but through this deliverance all the nations on earth will be converted and will turn to worship Yahweh: "All the ends of the world / Shall remember and turn to the LORD, / And all the families of the nations / Shall worship before You." In a moment, humiliation and defeat is transformed into radiant victory, with glorious worldwide consequences.

Psalm 41 vibrates with the same smarting sense of betrayal as Psalm

22. Here the psalmist laments that in his sickness, his enemies "speak evil against him," saying spitefully among themselves, "When will he die, and his name perish?" They were full of hypocrisy. They visited him on his sickbed, and then went out to share bad news with malevolent joy: "An evil disease . . . clings to him. / And *now* that he lies down, he will rise up no more." His closest friend, one with whom he had shared table fellowship (a strong and sacred bond in the Middle East), joined those who kicked him when he was down. "Even my own familiar friend in whom I trusted, / Who ate my bread, / Has lifted up *his* heel against me." And here again the psalm ends on a hopeful note. "By this I know that You are well pleased with me," he says to God, "because my enemy does not triumph over me. / As for me, You uphold me in my integrity, / And set me before Your face forever."

    Psalm 69 also echoes these cries of betrayal. The psalmist sees himself besieged with unjust accusers: "Though I have stolen nothing, / I *still* must restore *it*." His persecutors' insults and "reproach has broken my heart." He "looked *for someone* to take pity, but *there was* none; / And for comforters, but I found none." On the contrary, when he was hungry, his tormentors "gave me gall for my food, / And for my thirst they gave me vinegar to drink." But all would be well. God would judge his foes, so that their festal table would "become a snare before them" and "no one live in their tents." As for him, he would "praise the name of God with a song, / And will magnify Him with thanksgiving." The triumph would not be for him alone: God would "save Zion / and build the cities of Judah" as He restored His people.

    In **Psalm 109** we meet the same spiteful enmity and opposition to the House of David as in the previous two psalms. From the king's foes, "the mouth of the wicked and the mouth of the deceitful / Have opened against me;" they have "surrounded me with words of hatred." What made such hatred hardest to endure was that it was entirely unjustified. Despite being offered "love" by David, they still acted as his accusers and "rewarded me evil for good." The king was afflicted; his "heart is wounded within" him, he was "like a shadow when it lengthens," ready to fade away. He has "become a reproach to them"; when they see him, they "shake their heads" in contempt and mockery. They "persecuted the poor and needy man, / That he might even slay the broken in heart." The psalmist prays that God reward his foe as he deserved: "Let his days be few, / *And* let another take his office." The psalmist expects final vindication from God, and concludes on a note of praise: "I will greatly praise the LORD with my mouth; / Yes, I will praise Him among the multitude. / For He shall stand at the right hand of the poor, / To save *him* from those who condemn him."

To be sure, David's life had its full share of unjust opposition, spiteful enmity, heartbreak, and betrayal. His public career began with him being unjustly persecuted by King Saul, to whom he was always loyal and whom he always served faithfully (1 Sam. 19; 24; 28). He was further betrayed by Doeg the Edomite, one of Saul's men (1 Sam. 21—22). From his own family, David was betrayed by his beloved son Absalom (2 Sam. 15—19) and forced to flee for his life (2 Sam. 15). On the way he was cursed by Shimei, one of his subjects (2 Sam. 16). In his old age, his son Adonijah proclaimed himself king, in defiance of David's will, in a sudden palace coup. David was no stranger to betrayal.

Yet even so, the poetry of these psalms exceeds anything in David's personal history. The words represent a man utterly abandoned, as David never was (even during the lowest points of his life, he was still supported by his loyal retainers and friends). And not only did David's personal experience never plumb the depths of despair and desertion portrayed in the psalms, his vindication never reached the heights portrayed there either. David's personal crises ended with his being restored to his throne, but this restoration had no such global significance as we find, for example, in Psalm 22:27, for at no time in David's career did all the families of the earth turn to worship the Lord as a result of observing David's change of fortunes. In the psalms' portrayal of both the king's descent and his reascent, the sacred poetry overreaches any of the events of the tenth century BC.

The final days of Jesus of Nazareth compel us to read those psalms as the story of His suffering and betrayal. The words still remain poetry, not prediction (Christ never lay abandoned on a sickbed, for example, as in Ps. 41:3), but the poetry portrays His suffering and experiences with a vividness not to be denied. It reads, in fact, like a script of His

The Writings

Passion, with individual details bearing an eerily exact resemblance to His experiences.

Christ was sold out by one of His own inner circle, a close friend whom He trusted, one who ate His own bread and then went out from the table to betray Him to His death (John 13:21-30). In Gethsemane, He prayed with agony, afflicted and despondent in heart (Matt. 26:36-38). Not only that, but all of His disciples forsook Him and fled, so that He looked for comforters, but found none (Matt. 26:56). At His trial before the Sanhedrin, many false witnesses accused Him, opening a wicked and deceitful mouth against Him (Matt. 26:59-60). When Judas His betrayer saw that He had been condemned, he felt remorse for his deed, and went away and hanged himself, so that his days were few and his office of apostleship was taken by another (Matt. 27:5; Acts 1:15-26).

Christ's foes who conspired to deliver Him to Pilate's sentence of crucifixion had no reason for such enmity, for He had only ever done them good, so that in return for His love they acted as His accusers, repaying Him evil for good. The crowd assembled before Pilate entirely disowned Him, asking instead for Barabbas, as Christ was despised by the people (Matt. 27:20-23). After His condemnation by Pilate, He was nailed to a cross, and the soldiers pierced His hands and feet (John 19:18).

On the cross, He found Himself surrounded by a band of evildoers (Matt. 27:38-39) who mocked His pain, saying, "He trusted in God; let Him deliver Him now if He will have Him" (Matt. 27:41-43), wagging their heads in contempt (Matt. 27:39). The soldiers guarding Him took away His very clothes, casting lots for them to decide what piece each soldier would take (John 19:23-24). When He hung on the Cross, He was given gall (Matt. 27:34), and for His thirst was given vinegar (Matt. 27:48). In His final minutes, He cried out as did the psalmist, "My God, My God, why have You forsaken Me?" (Matt. 27:46). Three days later, God raised Him triumphantly from the dead, and through His Gospel, all the ends of the families of the nations have worshipped before God (Matt. 28:19).

In short, the significance of these psalms of betrayal written in the tenth century BC was only fully understood after Christ's Passion, when the grid of His final days was placed over the ancient poems.

Proverbs and the Wisdom of God

The Book of Proverbs is a collection of many aphorisms and pithy sayings, each one of which is meant to be pondered and savored. In the heart of the collection we find a poem extolling the divine wisdom. It is not the only personification of wisdom in the collection, but it contains the longest sustained metaphor of wisdom as a woman, existing before the creation of the world, sharing God's eternity.

In part, it reads:

> "The LORD possessed me at the beginning of His way,
> Before His works of old.
> I have been established from everlasting,
> From the beginning, before there was ever an earth.
> When *there were* no depths I was brought forth,
> When *there were* no fountains abounding with water.
> Before the mountains were settled,
> Before the hills, I was brought forth;
> While as yet He had not made the earth or the fields,
> Or the primal dust of the world.
> When He prepared the heavens, I *was* there,
> When He drew a circle on the face of the deep,
> When He established the clouds above,
> When He strengthened the fountains of the deep,
> When He assigned to the sea its limit,
> So that the waters would not transgress His command,
> When He marked out the foundations of the earth,
> Then I was beside Him *as* a master craftsman;
> And I was daily *His* delight,
> Rejoicing always before Him,
> Rejoicing in His inhabited world,
> And my delight *was* with the sons of men." (Prov. 8:22–31)

In this passage, the wisdom with which God created the world is personified as a woman, the Lady Wisdom. Why a woman (especially given that Yahweh is a god, not a goddess)? It is unlikely that the gender of the personified wisdom is simply due to the fact that the Hebrew noun for wisdom (*hokma*) is a feminine noun. Of more significance is the homiletical comparison between folly and wisdom found in Proverbs 9. In this chapter, Lady Wisdom appeals to all:

> "Whoever *is* simple, let him turn in here!"
> *As for* him who lacks understanding, she says to him,
> "Come, eat of my bread
> And drink of the wine I have mixed.
> Forsake foolishness and live,
> And go in the way of understanding." (Prov. 9:4–6)

Contrasting with this is the rival and alternative call of Lady Folly, who sends out her own appeal, saying, "Whoever *is* simple, let him turn in here . . . / Stolen water is sweet, / And bread *eaten* in secret is pleasant" (Prov. 9:16–17). By "water" and "bread" she does not mean groceries, but sex. Folly is personified as a woman because the author of Proverbs is warning against the folly of adultery. One has the choice of which "woman" to heed—wisdom or folly.

Wisdom guards against folly, for it will "deliver you from the immoral woman, / From the seductress *who* flatters with her words, / Who forsakes the companion of her youth" (Prov. 2:16–17). "Say to wisdom, 'You *are* my sister,' / And call understanding *your* nearest kin, / That they may keep you from the immoral woman, / From the seductress *who* flatters with her words" (Prov. 7:4–5). Wisdom bids a man, "Drink water from your own cistern, / And running water from your own well. . . . For why should you, my son, be enraptured by an immoral woman, / And be embraced in the arms of a seductress?" (Prov. 5:15, 20).

Such folly can indeed be tempting and alluring. But the author counsels the righteous to heed a different call—that of wisdom.

> Wisdom calls aloud outside;
> She raises her voice in the open squares.
> She cries out in the chief concourses,
> At the openings of the gates in the city
> She speaks her words:

"How long, you simple ones, will you love simplicity?
For scorners delight in their scorning,
And fools hate knowledge.
Turn at my rebuke;
Surely I will pour out my spirit on you;
I will make my words known to you." (Prov. 1:20–23)

Here we see wisdom's divine origin, for wisdom offers to pour out her Spirit in the same way that God speaks of pouring out His Spirit (Is. 32:15; 44:3; Joel 2:28). Lady Wisdom is thus not an *hypostasis* separate from God, but a metaphor for the Lord in His appeal to men. The passage in Proverbs 8:22f contains God's call to respond to His Law and walk wisely in the world. It says that wisdom is eternal, for through it, God made the world. This passage proclaims that the wisdom found in the Law was not simply a cultural code peculiar to a particular time and place, but something timeless, eternal, transcending all cultures. The personification of wisdom in this passage draws a connecting line from the eternal creative power by which God made the world to the demands of His Law which He gave on Mount Sinai. The lesson is clear: By keeping the Law and heeding the call of ethical wisdom, one participates in and conforms to an eternal norm.

The same image and lesson is found elsewhere in the Scriptures. In the Book of Baruch, the author says that God "traced out the whole way to knowledge and gave her to Jacob His servant. Afterward she appeared upon earth and lived among men" (Bar. 3:36–37). We note again the feminine gender of knowledge. God "traced out" the way of knowledge when He created the world, and then gave this "knowledge" to Jacob when He called him into covenant with Himself. "Afterward," (that is, on Mount Sinai), "she appeared on earth" in the form of the Law. Here we find the same metaphor of divine wisdom as a woman, which wisdom is offered to Israel through the Law. (Note: The *Orthodox Study Bible* has the reading, "He was seen upon the earth," reading the pronoun as a masculine.)

Greek philosophy would postulate a principle of reason and rationality, a *logos*, underpinning everything. For the Hellenized Jew Philo of Alexandria, (born 20 BC), the *logos* was the mind or reason of God, God in His rational aspect. The complicated connection between Stoicism and the thought of Philo is not one we can examine here, but it is fair to say the philosophical *logos* of Philo had much in common with the homiletical Wisdom of Proverbs 8:22. It is this commonality that allows us to read John's Gospel with its affirmation of Jesus as the incarnation of the divine *Logos* and make a connection between Christ and Solomon's personification of Wisdom. This identification is all the easier because Paul spoke of Christ as the "wisdom of God" (1 Cor. 1:24, 30). Also, Proverbs 8:22 spoke of Wisdom being with God at the creation of the world and as the instrument of that creation, and St. Paul affirmed that God had created the world through Christ (1 Cor. 8:6). Thus, we read the passages in Proverbs (and Baruch) as intimations of God's eternal Word, who would one day be incarnate in the Man Christ Jesus.

Job and the Vindication of Suffering

The story of Job is traditionally based on the life of Jobab, king of Edom, mentioned in Genesis 36:33. (This ascription is also reflected in the final verses of the book as found in the Septuagint.) The tale of Job contains some of the best poetry ever written, and it recounts the suffering of a man who suffers unjustly, though he is completely righteous. His acquaintances (famous proverbially as "Job's comforters") assume his great suffering proves he has committed a great sin, but Job continues to deny it and to insist on his innocence. At the end of the story, God appears on the scene in a whirlwind to confound the worldly "wisdom" of Job's tormenting "comforters," reveal His power, and show the folly of supposing human wisdom is adequate to question the providence of God. He then restores to Job all that he has lost. A Septuagintal addition to the Hebrew text adds, "It is written that he will rise with those whom the Lord resurrects" (Job 42:18 OSB). Suffering leads eventually to resurrection.

We read the story of Job as a model of the sufferings of Christ, a foreshadowing of His Passion and Resurrection. Like Job, Christ was innocent yet suffered greatly. Like Job, Christ was vindicated by God at His Resurrection. Along with the story of Joseph the patriarch, the tale of Job reveals that in this age God's chosen ones suffer unjustly. That the

Messiah, "the Righteous One,"[9] would suffer on a cross does not defy historical precedent. A crucified Christ is not a contradiction in terms. God's servants have always suffered unjustly and been misunderstood by their "pious" contemporaries before being vindicated by God. It is for this reason that the Book of Job is read in church at the Presanctified Liturgies during Holy Week.

The Song of Songs and the Love of the King

One of the most surprising inclusions in the canon of Scripture is the Song of Songs, long ascribed to Solomon. It consists of a series of erotic love poems, in which a man and a woman address one another in tenderness and mutual delight. Neither person is identified in the text, but traditional interpretation identifies the man as King Solomon (compare Songs 3:6–11) and the woman as his beloved bride. The content is more ideal than autobiographical, since the man clearly is romantically smitten with the woman so that he belongs to her alone, whereas Solomon had seven hundred wives and three hundred concubines (1 Kin. 11:3). The poems celebrate human love and sexuality, as the lovers rejoice in each other's physical charms with a wealth of multisensory imagery and double entendres, beginning their examinations of each other's physical features at the head and working their way down.

It has always been the conviction of Christians that such human love finds its ultimate root in God. God's love is the original, the prototype, and human love is the derivative, the copy. Our human love for God and for one another is a reflection of His love. God is the ultimate lover of mankind, and humanity is His beloved. He is the seeker, we are the sought. He is the bridegroom, we are the bride. That is why all true forms of mysticism portray the soul as feminine. It is also why some Jewish interpretations of the Song of Solomon saw in the king's love for his bride the love of Yahweh for Israel.

St. Paul reflected on the story of the creation of mankind as male and female in the Book of Genesis. That story proclaimed that the man "shall leave his father and mother and be joined to his wife, and they

---

9   A messianic title; compare Acts 7:52; 22:14; 1 John 2:1.

shall become one flesh" (Gen. 2:24). For St. Paul, the creation of Adam and Eve and their becoming one flesh in marriage contains a revelation of hidden realities (that is, a *mysterion,* see Eph. 5:32)—the unity of Christ being one flesh with us, His people. Just as Adam was one flesh with Eve, his bride, so Christ is one flesh with His bride, the Church. The deep mystery of human sexuality hides the deeper mystery of the love of Christ. Reading the Song of Songs, we see in the tenderness and devotion of the two partners a reflection and promise of Christ's love for us. It is perhaps not surprising that both the Song of Songs and the Book of Revelation end the same way, with the bride calling upon her bridegroom to return. "Make haste, my beloved, / And be like a gazelle / Or a young stag / On the mountains of spices" (Song 8:14). "Amen. Even so, come, Lord Jesus" (Rev. 22:20).

The Book of Daniel: Tales of Perseverance and Visions of Restoration

The Book of Daniel consists of a series of gripping tales and exciting visions. The center of emotional resonance is, I suggest, found in Daniel's prayer in chapter 9. The prophet Jeremiah had predicted that Israel's estrangement from God would last seventy years (Dan. 9:2), and now that the appointed period of punishment was coming to an end, Daniel prayed that God would restore Jerusalem and its Temple, that Israel might again have communion with God. In response, an angel told Daniel that the wait for the Temple's full and final restoration and for the appointed time of blessing on Israel would not be seventy years, but seventy *weeks* of years—i.e. a much longer time than Daniel had anticipated. Until then, Israel must steel itself for difficulty and persecution, trusting in God's sovereignty.

The tales of Daniel all reflect this necessity of perseverance under persecution. In chapter 1, Daniel and his three companions all refuse the defiling food provided for them in the performance of their government duties, and are rewarded for their refusal by God. In chapter 3, Daniel's companions refuse to worship the idolatrous image of Nebuchadnezzar even under threat of death. They are therefore cast alive into a fiery furnace, but are rescued by God. Chapter 4 presents Nebuchadnezzar himself as repenting of his idolatrous pride and being humbled by God. In chapter 5 we read of God's judgment on Nebuchadnezzar's successor Belshazzar and his kingdom as God writes a sentence of doom upon the wall, Daniel being the only one present able to read the supernatural script. In chapter 6 Daniel refuses to abstain from prayer to God or to pray to the king instead, as the king's law commands him. He is therefore punished by being thrown into the lions' den, but is rescued by God.

Each of these tales reveals how God judges the idolatrous nations and rescues His people when they resist the idolatry these nations demand. The necessity of perseverance under hostile foreign threat is the thread binding all these tales into one. It is also, in fact, the lesson learned through fire and persecution by Israel in the Maccabean resistance to Antiochus Epiphanes in the mid-second century BC.

This Antiochus Epiphanes features in the visions as "the little horn" (e.g. Dan. 8:9), the one who would "persecute the saints of the Most High" (Dan. 7:25) as grimly recounted in 4 Maccabees, and who defiled the Temple, making sacrifice impossible for "two thousand three hundred days" (Dan. 8:14). The full restoration of Jerusalem's peace and her Temple worship would have to await his destruction. Only then could the prophet Jeremiah's foretold time of restoration begin. The visions of Daniel all look forward to this final and glorious restoration. After a succession of empires (presented in the visions of chapters 2 and 7) would come the final empire, the Kingdom of God, in which God's people would enjoy His peace and blessing.

The turmoil among the nations of the world which would lead up to this final victory is recounted in detail in the final vision of chapters 10—12. It would be turmoil indeed—"a time of trouble, / Such as never was since there was a nation, / *Even* to that time" (Dan. 12:1). But the glorious end would surely come. Daniel would not live to see it, and so he must seal up his visions until the end time, when they would be fulfilled. But he would have his reward. He would "arise to your inheritance at the end of the days" (Dan. 12:13).

As Christians, we have been taught that we live in the end times (compare 1 Cor. 10:11), and persecution has always been the Church's lot. Thus we can hardly fail to see in these tales and visions relevance to our own story.

The Stone Cut Without Hands: Daniel 2

In the first vision of the Book of Daniel, Nebuchadnezzar is troubled by a dream. He dreams of a multi-metallic statue of himself, a statue with his own face. A stone was cut from a quarry supernaturally "without hands," and it "struck the image on its feet." Immediately the entire statue crumbled to bits and was swept away by the wind. The stone that struck the statue, however, grew in size until it was "a great mountain and filled the whole earth" (Dan. 2:34–35). Not unnaturally Nebuchadnezzar is alarmed, for he feels this is no ordinary dream, but an omen sent by God.

What Nebuchadnezzar fears, of course, is political assassination, since he dreamt that a statue of himself had been destroyed and supplanted by the stone that destroyed it. Not knowing whom to trust, he calls the soothsaying priests of his court and demands to know the meaning of the dream. (He is perhaps looking for the identity of the assassin.) To ensure their loyalty and that their interpretation comes from God (and not from the hidden assassin), he refuses to tell them the details of the dream in advance. God will know both the details and the interpretation, and if they are really guided by God (and not in the pay of the assassin), they will be able to relate the dream and its meaning.

The priests are aghast, especially since the offer of reward for correct interpretation is backed up by the threat of death for failure. They flatly refuse, saying no soothsayer on earth could accede to such an unreasonable demand. According to the tale, the royal decree then goes forth: All the court soothsayers are to be killed, presumably because they are in league with the assassin. The court soothsayers, of course, include Daniel.

Daniel does not panic, but trusts in God (a model of serenity for God's people under threat of persecution). Though pagan men may be nonplussed, Daniel knows the true God of heaven, who can reveal all things. In response to Daniel's prayer, God reveals the matter to him in a night vision.

Daniel therefore relates to the king the details of his dream, as well as its meaning. The multi-metallic nature of the statue means that after Nebuchadnezzar's empire, other empires will follow, each one inferior to its predecessor. The golden kingdom of Nebuchadnezzar's Babylon will be followed by a silver kingdom, then a bronze one, then one of iron, then a weak one of iron mixed with clay. Nebuchadnezzar's empire is therefore the head of all earthly empires, and none of the empires that follow will be able to compare with it.

At length, all these kingdoms will be destroyed by the power of God, symbolized in the dream by a stone supernaturally quarried without human hands. This kingdom of God will overthrow the inferior kingdom of iron and clay, and grow in power until it is like a great mountain, filling all the earth. In the distant days of one of those kings, "the God of heaven will set up a kingdom which shall never be destroyed; and the kingdom shall not be left to other people; it shall break in pieces and consume all these kingdoms, and it shall stand forever" (Dan. 2:44).

The king is elated, since this interpretation means assassination is not imminent, and his own life and sovereignty seem to be secure. In an act of extraordinary self-abasement, he bows down and does obeisance to Daniel. He also rewards him with promotion over the whole province of Babylon and over the other soothsayers (vv. 46–48).

Israel reading about this dream and its interpretation took great comfort. After the exile, empire succeeded empire, and yet the glory promised by the prophets was still nowhere to be seen. This dream meant those empires would eventually pass away, and the long-awaited Kingdom of God would come.

As we Christians read about this dream, we think of the Kingdom of God brought by Christ. Daniel said that "in the days of these kings, the God of heaven will set up a kingdom," and for Christians living in the Roman Empire, this could only mean the Kingdom brought in by Christ during their days. The dream foretold that the instrument bringing this Kingdom would be "a stone cut out without hands"—i.e. something endued with supernatural power. What else could this be but Christ, who was born without human seed, by the supernatural power of God? Christ's birth from a virgin fit the image exactly. His Mother was the uncut mountain, the quarry from which Christ was "cut without hands" by the power of the Holy Spirit. The Kingdom He brought, small as a mustard seed though it was during the days of His flesh, was destined to grow into a great tree, large enough that the birds of heaven could find shelter in its branches (Matt. 13:31–32; see

Ezek. 17:23). The small stone would grow into a mighty mountain in the age to come and would fill the whole earth.

The Three Holy Youths in the Fiery Furnace: Daniel 3

In chapter 3 we find the tale of Daniel's three friends and colleagues, who lived in Babylon under the names Shadrach, Meshach, and Abednego. Nebuchadnezzar made a gold image of himself ninety feet tall and commanded all the civil servants of the land to come and worship it. Everyone did so except the three Jewish friends of Daniel. Nebuchadnezzar's soothsayers, when they learn of this, denounce the three young men to the king, who hauls Shadrach, Meshach, and Abednego before him and repeats his demand that they worship the idol. If they continue in their refusal to worship, they will be cast into the midst of a fiery furnace and incinerated. "And who *is* the god," the king asks, "who will deliver you from my hands?" (Dan. 3:15). Thus the showdown is set up between the pagan king and the God of Israel.

The three holy youths remain defiant and are therefore bound and cast into the midst of the fiery furnace.

> Then King Nebuchadnezzar was astonished; and he rose in haste *and* spoke, saying to his counselors, "Did we not cast three men bound into the midst of the fire?"
>
> They answered and said to the king, "True, O king."
>
> "Look!" he answered, "I see four men loose, walking in the midst of the fire; and they are not hurt, and the form of the fourth is like the Son of God." (Dan. 3:24–25)

The comic element of the king's shock should not be missed, as God makes a fool out of the powerful king who has defied Him.

When the three youths are retrieved from the furnace, they are found to be completely untouched by the flame, with not even the smell of fire upon them. The king cries out, "Blessed be the God of Shadrach, Meshach, and Abed-Nego, who sent His Angel and delivered His servants who trusted in Him!" He goes on to command that any irreverence spoken against the Jewish God will from then on be punishable by a gruesome death, accompanied by the destruction of the homes of the offenders (Dan. 3:28–29).

The tale functioned to encourage the Jews who suffered under foreign and idolatrous regimes (such as those suffering under the pagan king Antiochus Epiphanes). It also functioned to encourage the Christians who suffered for Christ in the persecutions under the Romans. This tale exhorted Jews and Christians alike to persevere in their refusal to worship idols or to conform to the paganism surrounding them, even if this refusal was to cost their very lives.

Also, we cannot fail to notice the mode of rescue of the three holy youths—the presence with them in the fire of one "like a son of the gods" (*bar-elahin*; in Greek, *uios theou*, "a son of God"). In the original text of Daniel, the pagan king identifies this supernatural interloper as a divine angel sent by God. The phrase "a son of the gods" (note the plural "gods") simply denotes the being's heavenly, supernatural status. In the Greek translation, this phrase becomes "a son of God" (note the singular "God"). The change is the translator's transposition of a pagan idiom into a Jewish one, for the phrase "a son of God" still denoted an angel (compare the reference to angels as "sons of God" in Job 1:6).

But the resemblance of the phrase "a son of God" to the designation of Christ as "the Son of God" was too striking for Christians to ignore. The phrase does not mean that it was the preincarnate Son of God who was with the three holy youths in the furnace. The pagan Nebuchadnezzar would have no such understanding, and from a Christian perspective, the divine Logos could not be properly designated simply as God's angel. The word "angel" in the Book of Daniel and in exilic and postexilic literature always referred to one of God's created messengers. The title was never applied to God Himself.

Nonetheless, the reference to the supernatural rescuer as "a son of God" and the resemblance of the title to that of Christ could not be simply accidental. As in the days of King Ahaz the sign of God's presence was a *parthenos* conceiving and bearing a son, so here the title of the savior is "a son of God." The use of both images and titles is providential and prophetic. The messenger sent to protect the three holy youths in the furnace may not have been the preincarnate Logos, but he was certainly a type, a foreshadowing of the Son of God. Christian poetry rightly regards the presence of the *uios theou* in the furnace as an assurance that Christ will be with His disciples in their times of suffering. Whenever Christians undergo persecution or are cast headlong into their own furnaces of pagan fury, they can be assured that Christ will not abandon them, but will be with them to strengthen them and to bring them safely to the Kingdom.

The Son of Man Coming with the Clouds of Heaven: Daniel 7

In Daniel 7, we find what is possibly the most important of Daniel's visions of restoration, that of the four bestial kingdoms and the kingdom of the son of man. The term "son of man," of course, simply means "a human being." It refers to man in his humility, his weakness, his vulnerability (contrasted with the immortal angels, the "sons of God"). Thus the prophet Ezekiel is called "son of man" (e.g. Ezek. 2:1) as he trembles in weakness before his glorious Lord, who has revealed Himself in theophanic splendor (Ezek. 1).

This vision in Daniel contrasts the irrational and bestial nature of the pagan empires with the rational and humane nature of God's kingdom. The first empire, symbolized by a lion, refers to the Babylonian empire. It is followed by bestial empires symbolized by a bear, a leopard, and a nameless nightmarish creature with ten horns. The son of man symbolizes the kingdom in which "the saints of the Most High shall receive the kingdom, and possess the kingdom forever" (Dan. 7:18). Even as the four beasts symbolize four successive pagan kingdoms, so the human being symbolizes the Kingdom of God.

The moment of transfer of world power from this succession of bestial empires to that of "the saints of the Most High" coincides with the overthrow of the "little horn" who had "a mouth speaking pompous words," who had been "making war against the saints, and prevailing against them" (Dan. 7:8, 21). "The Ancient of Days came [i.e. the old one], and a judgment was made *in favor* of the saints of the Most High, and the time came for the saints to possess the kingdom" (v. 22). This transition is symbolized by a vision of a Son of Man.

> "I [Daniel] watched till thrones were put in place,
> And the Ancient of Days was seated;
> His garment *was* white as snow,
> And the hair of His head *was* like pure wool.
> His throne *was* a fiery flame,
> Its wheels a burning fire;
> A fiery stream issued
> And came forth from before Him. . . .
> The court was seated,
> And the books were opened.

> "I watched then because of the sound of the pompous words which the horn was speaking; I watched till the beast was slain, and its body destroyed . . .

> "I was watching in the night visions,
> And behold, *One* like the Son of Man,
> Coming with the clouds of heaven!
> He came to the Ancient of Days,
> And they brought Him near before Him.
> Then to Him was given dominion and glory and a kingdom,
> That all peoples, nations, and languages should serve Him."
> (Dan. 7:9–14)

In this vision, God in His heavenly power passed judgment on the "little horn," destroying the kingdom that was his. Then "one like a son of man" (i.e. one bearing the likeness of a human being, contrasting with the beasts who were in power before him) ascended to God's throne, brought there on the clouds of heaven. He approached God and was welcomed by Him. God gave to him the kingdom that had formerly been possessed by the fourth beast, whom God's judgment had just destroyed.

The son of man clearly symbolizes the saints of the Most High. Yet in the years after the Book of Daniel gained currency in Israel, the image of the son of man came to be regarded as a messianic figure, the Messiah in whom the saints of the Most High would receive the kingdom from God. Thus we read in the Book of Enoch (a composite volume, parts of which date from the second and first centuries before Christ):

> And the Lord of spirits seated [the Chosen One] on the throne of His glory and the Spirit of righteousness was poured out upon him. And the word of his mouth slays all the sinners, and all the unrighteous are destroyed from before his face . . . they shall be downcast, and pain shall seize them when they see that Son of Man sitting on the throne of his glory. . . . For from the beginning the Son of Man was hidden and the Most High preserved him in the presence of His might, and revealed him to the chosen ones . . . and all the kings and those who rule the earth shall fall down before him on their faces and worship, and set their hope upon that Son of Man, and petition him and supplicate for mercy at his hands. (Enoch 62:2–9)

In this passage, the term "son of man" has clearly become a title for the Messiah.[10]

It is this title, "Son of Man," that Jesus chose out of other possible ones as His own favorite self-designation. The title "Son of David" savored too much of militarism and armed might (not surprisingly, since David had been a guerrilla fighter and continued to shed blood in wars when he had been made king; see 1 Chr. 28:3). The title "Christ" also had such military overtones. The title "Son of Man" spoke of authority with God, but of a heavenly and supernatural kind, without the military connotations that would gain the unwanted attention of the Romans.

Jesus always referred to Himself as "the Son of Man" during His ministry. And He referred to this very passage in Daniel 7 at His final trial. He remained silent in the face of a barrage of false accusations. It was only when the high priest adjured Him in the Name of the living God to tell them whether or not He claimed to be the Christ that He

---

10 The dating of parts of the Book of Enoch is problematic. It is possible that this passage has experienced Christian redaction. W. Oesterley dates it to no later than 64 BC.

replied, "*It is as* you said. Nevertheless, I say to you, hereafter you will see the Son of Man sitting at the right hand of the Power, and coming on the clouds of heaven" (Matt. 26:63–64). In this reply Christ cited Psalm 110:1 about the Messiah sitting at the right hand of God. He also cited this vision of Daniel 7:13, about the Son of Man coming on the clouds of heaven to God to receive the Kingdom from Him. The high priest and all who heard Jesus' reply recognized that He was indeed claiming to be the Messiah.

Our Lord's citation of this passage in Daniel directs us in our own interpretation of it. Jesus was the Son of Man, who at the Ascension came on the clouds to God's right hand and received the Kingdom from Him. In the words of Peter, "God has made this Jesus . . . both Lord and Christ" at His Ascension, when He received from God "all authority . . . in heaven and on earth" as His chosen Messiah (Acts 2:36; see Matt. 28:18). The bestial kingdoms of the earth, including those of Nebuchadnezzar and his successors in world power, had been replaced by the Kingdom of God.

The fulfillment of this vision partakes of the same depoliticization as the other prophecies of the Old Testament. The kingdoms of Nebuchadnezzar and of the nameless fourth beast ruled by the little horn had been earthly empires with boundaries, political sovereignty, and armies. Christ's Kingdom is not of this world. It has no boundaries, no political power, and needs no armies. Such heavenly transcendence makes it more secure, not less. Other kingdoms will rise and fall. This kingdom will endure forever. As Daniel's vision promised, "His dominion *is* an everlasting dominion, / Which shall not pass away, / And His kingdom *the one* / Which shall not be destroyed" (Dan. 7:14).

The Later Books: Hanging onto Hope

The later books (commonly called the "Apocrypha" by Protestants and the *Anaginoskomena* by Orthodox) share a common commitment to spiritual tenacity. They were written in the closing years of the era before Christ and later, a time when the Jewish people were under stress from the surrounding Gentile world. Accordingly, these books have a polemical purpose and tone, as the Chosen People defended their hope against the challenges of the paganism surrounding them.

First Esdras recounts the history of postexilic Israel and breathes an air of renewed hope, encouraging Israel to trust God in the midst of the challenges of living again in the land while surrounded by hostile powers. Second Esdras (a composite book, with chapters 1—2 and 15—16 being later additions) contains an apocalypse, in which the kingdoms of the world are finally dissolved in favor of the coming Kingdom of God. Like all apocalypses, it copes with the difficulties of the present age by directing readers' hopes to the age to come. (Anyone reading the Book of Revelation would benefit by familiarity with this book, since it helps one to understand the apocalyptic genre.)

The Book of Tobit recounts the pious tale of Tobias, who goes on a journey accompanied (unbeknownst to him) by an angel, who helps him fulfill his duty. The tale is replete with pious advice and underscores the importance of maintaining Jewish piety in a pagan world—including the importance of choosing a Jewish wife and not a pagan one.

The Book of Judith tells the story of the heroic Judith, who, at the risk of life and honor, deceives the brutal invading general Holofernes with her womanly wiles and assassinates him in his own tent. It is a tale of resistance and the value of courage in the face of Gentile aggression.

The Wisdom of Solomon is a series of poems meditating on the glories of the Law as the true wisdom of God for Israel. Faithfulness to Him (and resisting the blandishments of secular Greek wisdom) is the path that leads to life. The Book of Sirach (sometimes called "Ecclesiasticus" because it was a great favorite with the *ecclesia* or church) contains a collection of proverbs and pious advice. It attempts to preserve the traditional piety of Israel in the face of a rival secular Gentile wisdom and philosophy.

The Book of Baruch (purporting to be written by Jeremiah's assistant of that name) exhorts its readers to flee idolatry (i.e. temptations to paganism), since it was through idolatry that Israel fell and suffered exile in Babylon. Baruch also contains a series of prophecies, repeatedly exhorting the people to take courage and be faithful to God. Appended to Baruch is the so-called Letter of Jeremiah, a long denunciation of the folly of idolatry (or, in the historical context of its time, the folly of Hellenism). The additions to the Book of Daniel, particularly the story of Susanna and Bel and the Dragon (or serpent), are short stories illustrating the need for perseverance in righteousness and the folly of idols. In the story of Susanna, Daniel is a detective who clears the falsely accused Susanna of charges of immorality. Her vindication shows the importance of maintaining a pure lifestyle in the midst of pagan impurity. In the story of Bel and the Dragon, Daniel is again a detective who reveals to the king of Babylon the stupidity of idol worship and how the cult is based on lies. What these tales lack in historicity and nuance, they make up for in humor and polemic.

The Books of Maccabees (Orthodoxy recognizes four volumes) narrate the struggle between Judaism and Hellenism, and how God is on the side of His chosen people—an incentive to cling tenaciously to the old faithful ways.

The books in this varied collection were all written in the years when Israel felt itself under pressure from its contact with an aggressive and attractive Hellenism. Through the genres of short story, proverb, apocalypse, polemical denunciation, and historical narrative, they urge the people of God to hang onto their hope and not let the world squeeze them into its mold. He promised them His Kingdom, and they must remain firm in their hope if they are to inherit it.

The Shameful Death of God's Son: Wisdom 2

As an example of the value of these *Anaginoskomena*, we may examine a section in the second chapter of the Wisdom of Solomon. The ungodly (i.e. those influenced by Hellenism) rejected the old ways of Jewish faithfulness, and derided and even persecuted those who persisted in it. In this meditation, the secular cynics conspire together to "eat, drink, and be merry," embracing a life of callous self-indulgence, enriching themselves through exploiting the helpless. This exploitation does not stop at anything, including killing the man of integrity who gets in their way.

In this meditation, we read the following:

[The ungodly] said among themselves, as they reasoned
    incorrectly:
"Our life is short and painful,
And there is no cure for the death of a man . . .
When the spark is extinguished, our body will turn to ashes,
And our breath will disperse like empty air. . . .
Come, therefore, let us enjoy the good things that exist. . . .
Let us be filled with expensive wine and perfumes. . . .
Let us oppress the righteous poor man;
Let us not spare a widow. . . .
Let our might be our law of righteousness,
For what is weak is shown to be useless.
Let us lie in ambush for the righteous man,
Because he is useless to us and opposes our deeds;
He denounces us for our sins against the law
And accuses us of sins against our upbringing.
He claims to have knowledge of God,
And he calls himself a child of the Lord. . . .
Even seeing him is a burden to us. . . .
He considers the last things of the righteous as blessed
And pretends that God is his Father.
Let us see if his words are true,
And let us put these last things to the test at the end of
    his life.
For if the righteous man is a son of God, He will help him,
And deliver him from the hand of those who oppose him.
Let us test him with insult and torture
That we may know his gentleness
And test his patient endurance.
Let us condemn him to a shameful death,
For there shall be a visitation because of his words."
So they reasoned these things
And were led astray,
For their malice blinded them.
    (Wisdom 2:1–21 OSB)

As we read these words, we cannot but apply them to our Lord. It is as if the entire course of the Lord's Passion were recorded in advance. As C. S. Lewis said of a similar passage in Plato about a righteous man being bound, scourged, and impaled (i.e. crucified), "A Christian reader starts and rubs his eyes," seeing the Passion of Christ accurately described in advance by Plato. "Plato is talking . . . about the fate of goodness in a wicked and misunderstanding world. But that is not something simply other than the Passion of Christ. It is the very same thing of which that Passion is the supreme illustration" (from his *Reflections on the Psalms*).

It is the same with this description in the Wisdom of Solomon of the shameful death by torture of God's Son. The ungodly who oppose God's Servant object to Him because He denounces them for their sins. The righteous man calls God His Father. The ungodly therefore conspire together to have Him condemned to a shameful death, so that the one who calls Himself the Son of God dies amid insult and torture. As Lewis said, this is not something other than the Passion of Christ. And because Jesus was the Son of God, His ungodly foes will find that "they were led astray."

CONCLUSION

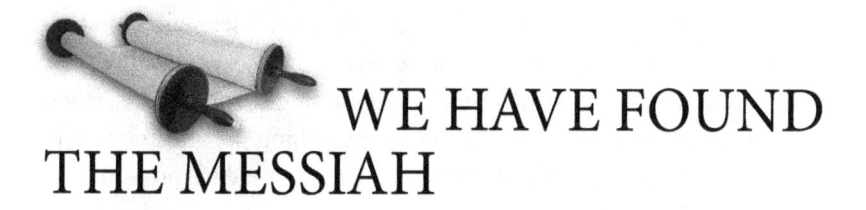

WE HAVE FOUND THE MESSIAH

The Case for the Christian Interpretation

AS WE HAVE SHOWN, the Christian interpretation of the Old Testament is not something the disciples of Christ ingeniously thought up and then arbitrarily read into the Hebrew Scriptures, as a kind of perverse partisan eisegesis. Rather, our Lord's disciples had the indelible and shattering experience of seeing the life of Jesus, and of partaking of salvation in the Church, and then seeing this life and salvation portrayed in the ancient Scriptures. They were not reading things into the texts, but discovering meanings they believed God had hidden there for them to find when Jesus had come. Thus, the Christian interpretation is inseparable from Christian experience. It follows that rejection of the Christian interpretation of the Old Testament involves rejection of the claims of Jesus.

Such rejection is possible, of course. One can look at the claims of Jesus to be one with the Father and to have divine authority to forgive sins and reject these claims as lies. One can look at the miracles of Jesus and assert that they were done by the power of the devil. This was the position of the Pharisees who opposed Jesus: "Do we not say rightly that You are a Samaritan and have a demon?" "By the ruler of the demons He casts out demons" (John 8:48; Mark 3:22). Rejecting Jesus as the Messiah, the Pharisees (and non-Christian interpretation after them) also rejected the Church's interpretation of the Hebrew Scriptures and denied that the ancient texts prophesied of Jesus and His Church.

There are, however, insuperable difficulties in maintaining this position. It is not simply the difficulty of dismissing pages upon pages of Old Testament text that find fulfillment in Jesus as astonishing coincidences. There is also the difficulty of squaring the ancient prophecies with Israel's history after the days of Jesus if He were not the Messiah.

For example, in AD 70, the Romans destroyed Jerusalem and its Temple, laying waste the Jewish state and sending thousands into exile. The early second century saw some final mopping-up operations, when the last dying embers of Jewish national sovereignty were stamped out. From that time, the people of the Jewish state were led captive among all nations. This was the greatest national disaster ever to befall the Jewish people.

The Hebrew Scriptures, however, speak of the time after Israel's return from the Babylonian captivity as a time of lasting security and glory. All the prophets spoke of this radiant future. For example, Isaiah said that when Israel was again in the land, God would defend them so that "no weapon formed against you shall prosper" (Is. 54:17). Jeremiah assured them that the people "shall come and sing in the height of Zion, / Streaming to the goodness of the LORD . . . Their souls shall be like a well-watered garden, / And they shall sorrow no more at all" (Jer. 31:12).

Ezekiel spoke of the time when God will "establish one shepherd over them, and he shall feed them—My servant David . . . they shall no longer . . . bear the shame of the Gentiles" (Ezek. 34:23, 29). According to Hosea, in that day, God "will be like the dew to Israel; . . . Those who dwell under his shadow shall return; / They shall be revived *like* grain, / And grow like a vine" (Hos. 14:5–7). Through Amos God promised, "I will plant them in their land, / And no longer shall they be pulled up / From the land I have given them" (Amos 9:15).

Micah echoed this promise, saying that Israel's Davidic King "shall stand and feed *His flock* / In the strength of the LORD, / In the majesty of the name of the LORD His God; / And they shall abide, / For now He shall be great / To the ends of the earth" (Micah 5:4). Zephaniah therefore counseled them, "Do not fear; / Zion, let not your hands be weak. / The LORD your God in your midst, / The Mighty One, will save" (Zeph. 3:16). Zechariah spoke of the divine wrath that would befall any who dared to invade God's people, saying, "And this shall be the plague with which the LORD will strike all the people who fought against Jerusalem: Their flesh shall dissolve while they stand on their feet" (Zech. 14:12).

This brief selection from the prophets provides abundant confirmation of the divine promise that after the return from the Babylonian captivity, God would raise up His Messiah and Israel would dwell in lasting peace and security, knowing the unshakable blessing of God.

If Jesus was not that Messiah, raised up after the return from exile, then the prophecies have proven a lie and a false hope. God promised through one prophet after another that the return from exile would not be followed by any more disaster for His people, and that they would never again be plucked up out of the land, but that after the return from exile He would send King Messiah.

Christians have asserted that Jesus, coming after the exile while Israel was in the land, was that King Messiah, and they interpret His Kingdom, prosperity, and peace in spiritual terms, not earthly political ones. But if that Christian interpretation be rejected, one is compelled to admit that God did *not* send His Messiah after Israel was back in the land, but rather that Israel was indeed plucked out of it. In other words, the stark choice is between the Christian interpretation and the admission that the scriptural hope was a delusion and its promises were in vain.

Another difficulty faces one who believes the Hebrew Scriptures while rejecting the Christian interpretation of them. The principle on which God dealt with His people, as far back as the days of Moses, was that obedience to God would be rewarded with blessing and security, and that disobedience would be punished with disaster and exile. When the prophets threatened Israel with exile if they persisted in their sins and idolatry, they were simply echoing the provisions and promises of the Mosaic covenant: "If you do not carefully observe all the words of this law... Then the LORD will scatter you among all peoples, from one end of the earth to the other" (Deut. 28:58, 64). The catastrophe of the Babylonian captivity of 586 BC was caused by Israel's grievous sin and persistent idolatry.

The question then arises: What sin caused the greater catastrophe of AD 70? That disaster was immeasurably greater than the earlier captivity, for the exile to Babylon only lasted a proverbial lifetime of seventy years (in actual calendar fact, from 586 BC to 520 BC, when Cyrus issued the decree allowing the return from exile). The blow that fell in AD 70 has lasted many more lifetimes, persisting through the centuries. Therefore, the sin causing it must have been that much greater.

What was that sin? What sin could Israel have committed that was immeasurably greater than the injustice and idolatry denounced by the preexilic prophets? The Christian answer is: the rejection and crucifixion of the Messiah. If one rejects that answer and explanation, one then needs to explain the cause of the AD 70 disaster in terms consistent with the covenantal promises of God in the Scriptures. The history of Israel after the days of Jesus also argues for the Christian interpretation of the Hebrew Scriptures as prophesying the life and power of Jesus, the Christ of God.

"Take Up and Read": The Riches of the Christian Interpretation

The divine Scriptures are a mine providing an inexhaustible supply of spiritual gold, and no single exegete or teacher can bring forth all the riches they offer. As Chrysostom once said, "It is a well that has no bottom." The prophecies of Jesus and the salvation He bestows in His Church were not hidden by God in the Old Testament simply to prove the point that Jesus is the Messiah. They do reveal the messiahship of Jesus, of course, but this is not their sole purpose. God gave the Scriptures for "doctrine, for reproof, for correction, for instruction in righteousness, that the man of God may be complete, thoroughly equipped for every good work" (2 Tim. 3:16–17). We are to feed on the rich fare provided in the Old Testament so that we may grow in spiritual strength and be ready for the work to which God calls us.

The scriptural passages examined in this volume are not presented as a complete collection of all the Old Testament prophecies of Christ and His Church, but as a representative handful of examples. Reading the works of the Fathers would disclose many more such examples, and we as the children of the Fathers will find others ourselves when we read. But we must read the Old Testament in its totality as *prophetikos*, as texts that were written with divine foreknowledge of Jesus. The Kingdom the prophetic texts promise is not an earthly Israelite kingdom (the theological error of "Christian Zionism"), but finds its fulfillment in the Church of Christ, as a comparison of all the New Testament citations of the Old Testament will show. As members of Christ's Church, we have these ancient texts as our inheritance, and we will be the poorer if we leave our inheritance unclaimed.

St. Augustine was once moved by the providence of God to "take up and read." He heard a young boy, in childish imitation of his teacher, repeating over and over again the chant, *"Tolle, lege! Tolle, lege!"* (Latin for "Take up and read!"). On impulse, he took up the nearest book and began to read the words of St. Paul from Romans 13:13–14: "Let us walk properly, as in the day, not in revelry and drunkenness, not in lewdness and lust, not in strife and envy. But put on the Lord Jesus Christ, and make no provision for the flesh, to *fulfill its* lusts."

The great saint confessed that he owed his conversion to this reading. Reading can bring the grace and power of God. St. Augustine and all the Fathers, East and West, knew this, and they encouraged the Church to read the Scriptures in order to grow in grace. Not all people in those old days possessed books, for books were very expensive. But books are not as expensive now, and any Christian in North America can easily own a copy of the Bible.

The Fathers encourage us to read the Scriptures of the Old Testament as children of the New, and to read them as much as possible. Indeed, spiritual growth is scarcely possible if we refuse to do so. The Hebrew Scriptures await our reading, promising insight, growth in Christ, and spiritual riches to any who read them with purity of heart and eagerness of spirit. Since we are the heirs of the Fathers, I encourage you to close this present volume, lay your hands on a copy of the Scriptures of the Old Testament, and take up and read.

About the Author

Archpriest Lawrence Farley currently pastors St. Herman of Alaska Orthodox Church (OCA) in Langley, B.C., Canada. He received his B.A. from Trinity College, Toronto, and his M.Div. from Wycliffe College, Toronto. A former Anglican priest, he converted to Orthodoxy in 1985 and studied for two years at St. Tikhon's Orthodox Seminary in Pennsylvania. He has also published *Let Us Attend: A Journey Through the Orthodox Divine Liturgy; Following Egeria: A Visit to the Holy Land through Time and Space; One Flesh: Salvation through Marriage in the Orthodox Church; The Empty Throne: Reflections on the History and Future of the Orthodox Episcopacy; Unquenchable Fire: The Traditional Teaching About Hell*, and the books in the Orthodox Bible Study Companion Series (see following page).

ANCIENT FAITH RADIO

Visit www.ancientfaith.com to read Fr. Lawrence Farley's blog, "No Other Foundation."

Books in the *Orthodox Bible Study Companion Series*

The Gospel of Matthew
Torah for the Church
- Paperback, 400 pages, ISBN 978-0-9822770-7-2

The Gospel of Mark
The Suffering Servant
- Paperback, 280 pages, ISBN 978-1-888212-54-9

The Gospel of Luke
Good News for the Poor
- Paperback, 432 pages, ISBN 978-1-936270-12-5

The Gospel of John
Beholding the Glory
- Paperback, 376 pages, ISBN 978-1-888212-55-6

The Acts of the Apostles
Spreading the Word
- Paperback, 352 pages, ISBN 978-1-936270-62-0

The Epistle to the Romans
A Gospel for All
- Paperback, 208 pages, ISBN 978-1-888212-51-8

First and Second Corinthians
Straight from the Heart
- Paperback, 319 pages, ISBN 978-1-888212-53-2

Words of Fire
The Early Epistles of St. Paul to the Thessalonians and the Galatians
- Paperback, 172 pages, ISBN 978-1-936270-02-6

The Prison Epistles
Philippians – Ephesians – Colossians – Philemon
- Paperback, 224 pages, ISBN 978-1-888212-52-5

Shepherding the Flock
The Pastoral Epistles of St. Paul the Apostle to Timothy and Titus
- Paperback, 144 pages, ISBN 978-1-888212-56-3

The Epistle to the Hebrews
High Priest in Heaven
- Paperback, 184 pages, ISBN 978-1-936270-74-3

Universal Truth
The Catholic Epistles of James, Peter, Jude, and John
- Paperback, 232 pages, ISBN 978-1-888212-60-0

The Apocalypse of St. John
A Revelation of Love and Power
- Paperback, 240 pages, ISBN 978-1-936270-40-8

Please visit our website for complete ordering information or to order online: store.ancientfaith.com.

We hope you have enjoyed and benefited from this book. Your financial support makes it possible to continue our non-profit ministry both in print and online. Because the proceeds from our book sales only partially cover the costs of operating **Ancient Faith Publishing** and **Ancient Faith Radio**, we greatly appreciate the generosity of our readers and listeners. Donations are tax-deductible and can be made at **www.ancientfaith.com.**

To view our other publications,
please visit our website: **store.ancientfaith.com**

ANCIENT FAITH RADIO

Bringing you Orthodox Christian music, readings, prayers, teaching, and podcasts 24 hours a day since 2004 at
www.ancientfaith.com